TBILISI

Stephen Stocks

CONTENTS

Foreword

Tbilisi has an irresistible charm that is neither European nor Asian, but rather a unique blend of cultural influences concocted over centuries of turbulent history. Some boldly assert that Tbilisi acts, not just as the capital of Georgia, but also as a capital for the entire Caucasus region. Of course, proud Azeris and Armenians would dispute this vociferously.

The fact remains that, for centuries, first-time visitors to the Caucasus made a beeline for Tbilisi before exploring any other city. John Steinbeck, who documented his 1948 travels in Russia in *A Russian Journal*, remarked: "The magical name of Georgia came up constantly. Indeed, we began to believe that most Russians hope that if they live good and virtuous lives, they will not go to heaven but to Georgia when they die'.

At the centre of Georgian life, Tbilisi lives up to its billing. Its setting is nothing short of dramatic, arrayed along the banks of the swiftly-flowing Mtkvari river, under the brooding battlements of Narikala fortress and the green slopes of Mtatsminda Park. In the old town, houses crowd the higgledy-piggledy alleyways, their ornate balconies jutting out precariously in varying degrees of decay. Centuries of religious tolerance becomes apparent when you stumble upon ancient churches, mosques, synagogues and even a

Tbilisi

Zoroastrian fire temple. Masseurs in sulphur bathhouses continue to scrub and pummel away, as they have done for centuries. Grand buildings line nineteenth-century boulevards, and everywhere the urban sprawl is broken up by leafy parks providing tired tourists with the chance to rest their weary feet. Neighbourhood bakeries and restaurants churn out endless supplies of khachapuri and khinkali, while cellars showcase their vintage Georgian wines.

Tbilisi offers an accessible, traveller-friendly infrastructure, with a wide selection of hotels and restaurants catering to every taste. Public transport stretches into every corner of the city, making it easy and cost-effective to see all the sights.

The city has come so far since Soviet times, and its development has accelerated even more after the Rose Revolution in 2003. The city is still not overrun with tourists, and many of the sights you'll have to yourself. And what's even better, the visa regime has been significantly relaxed, with many nationalities visa-exempt or eligible for e-visas. So now's the perfect time to visit, and this book will be your companion as you explore the city. Welcome to Tbilisi.

About this guide

This easy-to-use city guide helps you to unearth Tbilisi's treasures. Organised around a series of leisurely walking tours and some further afield excursions, you will get in-depth information on all buildings, statues, parks, markets, places of worship and any other point of interest, researched through personal visits and by drawing on the expertise of locals. Every step of the way, uncluttered easy-to-follow maps guide you around the city.

This book is organised in readily digestible chunks:

- *Getting to know Tbilisi* gives a brief history of the city and examines its history, geography and demographics.
- *Part 1* navigates north from Freedom Square and takes a walk up Tbilisi's grand thoroughfare, Rustaveli Avenue.
- *Part 2* wanders west of the Mtkvari river and explores the winding alleyways and ancient churches of Tbilisi's historical heart.
- *Part 3* steps south from Gorgasali Square to experience sulphur baths, hidden waterfalls and the lofty battlements of Narikala fortress.

Tbilisi

- **Part 4** crosses the river to the experience the atmospheric nineteenth-century streets of the east bank.
- **Part 5** goes further afield on a day trip from Tbilisi, to see the UNESCO World Heritage sights of Mtskheta, and Gori, the birthplace of Stalin.
- **Preparing for your visit** gives you all the essential practical information needed to make your trip plain sailing.

List of Maps

Here are the maps that feature in this guide:

Map A: Freedom Square to Georgian National Parliament
Map B: Georgian National Parliament to 9 April Park
Map C: 9 April Park to Tbilisi Funicular and Mount Mtatsminda
Map D: Rustaveli Theatre to Biltmore Hotel
Map E: Academy of Sciences to Rose Revolution Square
Map F: Gorgasali Square to Erekle II Street
Map G: Erekle II Street to Tbilisi Town Hall
Map H: Tbilisi Town Hall to Lado Gudiashvili Square
Map I: Lado Gudiashvili Square to Kote Afkhazi Street
Map J: Gorgasali Square to Orbeliani Baths
Map K: Orbeliani Baths to the Botanical Gardens
Map L: Botanical Gardens to Aerial Tram and Rike Park
Map M: Marjanishvili Square to Dry Bridge Market
Map N: Dry Bridge Market to St Trinity Cathedral
Map O: St Trinity Cathedral to Gorgasali Square

Getting to know Tbilisi

A brief history

The history of Tbilisi spans more than 1500 years and accordingly many myths swirl around its formation. The most popular of these describes how King Vakhtang Gorgasali was hunting in the woods along the banks of the Mtkvari river. He wounded a pheasant which subsequently dropped into one of the many hot springs in the area. The water had a miraculous curative effect, and the bird flew off to live another day. The king, amazed by the healing powers of the water, decided to move his capital here from Mtskheta forthwith. 'Tbili' in Georgian means warm, and so was an apt name for a settlement centred on so many hot springs.

It was the son of Vakhtang Gorgasali, King Dachi, who eventually succeeded in actually moving the capital to Tbilisi in the sixth century, and in building the all-important defences. However, the walls did not deter a procession of invading armies over the centuries, and by some accounts, there were forty separate conquests. Each time parts of Tbilisi were either destroyed or damaged and then renovated and rebuilt during intervening periods of peace. The result is a city with multiple layers of history, and many of the old buildings you see today are built on top, or from, much earlier structures.

From the sixth to the twelfth centuries, there were successive waves of Arab, Khazar, Seljuk Turk and Persian occupations. Then King David the Builder made his triumphal appearance, winning the city back and making it the capital once again of a united Georgia. He earnt his nickname from his ambitious renovation and construction projects throughout the city, and under his leadership, Tbilisi grew into a leading economic centre of the Caucasus. This was an enlightened golden age, during which the arts flourished, and Shota Rustaveli penned his most accomplished works.

Alas, as is the way in this part of the world, it did not last long, and darkness returned in the form of a crushing defeat at the hands of the Mongols in the thirteenth century. Turbulent times returned, and hostile forces repeatedly invaded the city. During the sixteenth to eighteenth centuries, the Persians and Turks generally held the upper hand, with the city experiencing great deprivations. It was not until 1748 that King Erekle II managed to drive the invaders out.

In the latter half of the eighteenth century, Georgia became the frontline of the Great Game between the Russia, Persian and Ottoman empires. Tbilisi had the unenviable task of deciding which power to support to secure its own best interests. Eventually, the rulers turned to Russia for support. However, this was not always forthcoming and invading Persians destroyed large segments of the city in 1795. Nevertheless, the country joined the Russian empire in 1800, signalling an end to the Royal family, and surrendering independence for the best part of two more centuries.

Under Russian rule, Tbilisi grew economically and politically. A significant amount of infrastructure was built, with new roads and railways connecting Tbilisi to other parts of the Caucasus and the Russian empire. New buildings were erected, and the city became a major cultural centre, with poets, artists and writers all coming to prominence during this time. At the turn of the century, Tbilisi played host to many anti-Tsarist revolutionaries, and it was here that Georgian Josef Stalin started out on his career. When the Tsarist regime eventually fell in 1918, Georgia declared independence, although a couple of years later was subsumed into the Soviet Union. Tbilisi and Georgia then waited another seventy years to feel the taste of freedom once more.

Geography

Tbilisi is Georgia's capital, situated in the southeast of the country. It is roughly equidistant from the borders with Azerbaijan and Armenia, both approximately forty to fifty kilometres away. The city is just above 41 degrees north and sits at an altitude of between 380 - 770 metres. Tbilisi is surrounded on three sides by various mountain ranges, and the Lori plain stretches away to the east.

The Mtkvari river dissects the city into two roughly equal parts. The oldest section is to the west of the river, and the dominant features here are the hills upon which the Narikala fortress and Mtatsminda Park are located. The main thoroughfare in this part of town is Rustaveli Avenue, lined by grand buildings of note. It links Freedom Square to Rose Revolution Square and the Vera and Vake neighbourhoods. The other side of the river is flatter and more regularly laid out. Here, Davit Aghmashenebli Avenue is the busiest street, lined with shops, restaurants and commerce of all types.

For most visitors, most sights of interest lie to the west of the river, although the eastern bank also has its highlights. The main tourist areas are bounded by the Botanical Gardens in the south, Vera Park in the north, Mtatsminda Park in the west, and St. Trinity Cathedral in the east.

Demographics

Just over 1.2 million people live in Tbilisi, which means that around a third of the entire Georgian population lives within its municipal limits. The city's population is likely to steadily rise over the coming decades as more people migrate to cities from the countryside. This growth contrasts with forecasts of a declining national population, primarily brought about by the economic situation putting downward pressure on family size.

While Tbilisi is overwhelmingly Georgian, the city still exudes a cosmopolitan atmosphere, with the biggest ethnic minorities, as you'd expect, being Russian, Azerbaijanis and Armenians. However, there are also Ukrainians, Greeks, Kurds, Yazidis and many others making up this melting pot.

The majority of people (84%) follow Georgian Orthodox Christianity. However, Georgia is famed for its long-held religious freedom and tolerance. Accordingly, you can find synagogues, mosques and a wide variety of churches serving Christian minorities.

Languages

Georgian is the official language, a Kartvelian tongue with a unique script, that is said to be one of the oldest languages still surviving today. It is spoken by 88% of citizens. The most popular second languages are Russian and English. You will probably find that older people are more likely to speak Georgian with quite fluent Russian, and youngsters will have a better grip of English. Interestingly, Georgian bears no resemblance to the languages of its neighbours, Azerbaijani and Armenian, and derives from an entirely different linguistic family.

PART 1 - *Navigating north from Freedom Square*

This walking tour begins at the very heart of Tbilisi, Freedom Square. Most hotels and other tourist accommodation should be within easy reach of this busy part of town. If you are staying a little further out, there is a red line metro station in the square. Many bus routes also stop here.

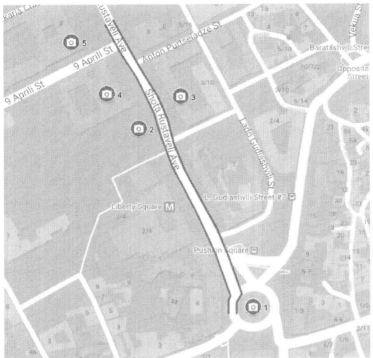

Map A: Freedom Square to Georgian National Parliament

Key:
  1. Freedom Square
  2. Garden of the First National Republic
  3. Georgia National Museum
  4. Viceroy's (Vorontsov's) Palace
  5. Georgian National Parliament

Freedom Square

Freedom Square *(Map A, Point 1)* dates back to the beginning of the nineteenth century, the time when the grand Rustaveli Avenue was also laid out. Its original name was Paskevich Square, honouring a victorious general of the Russian Empire. It was renamed Freedom Square when the country declared independence in 1918, although during most of the Soviet Union days it was referred to as Lenin Square.

The most prominent feature is a tall column at the top of which is a gilded statue of St. George on horseback. This is dedicated to the liberty and independence of the Georgian people and replaced a loathed Lenin monument that stood for years on the same spot.

Freedom Square has been the site of many national celebrations and also demonstrations; it's the focal point of the country. In an infamous incident in 2005, there was an attempted assassination attempt on US President George W Bush when a protestor threw a live hand grenade at the visiting leader. Thankfully, it failed to go off!

Garden of the First Republic of Georgia

As you walk up Rustaveli Avenue, on the left-hand side, look out for the wrought iron railings which form the elegant entrance to the Garden of the First Republic of Georgia *(Map A, Point 2)*. This private garden of the adjacent palace was the exclusive preserve of the elite.

The garden was extensively renovated and redesigned in the mid-eighteenth century by Swedish architect Ottom Jacob Simonson, and the layout you see today is mostly his work. He also added the grand staircase leading up to the shady terrace of the adjacent Vorontsov Palace (see below). Politicians signed the Independence Act in this palace in 1918, hence the name of the garden.

If you are a keen horticulturalist, there are some rare species of plant to look out for here, including the red pine, Chinese flowering chestnut, bleeding heart and white fir.

Georgian National Museum

Opposite the Garden of the First Republic is the Georgian National History Museum *(Map A, Point 3)*. This early twentieth-century building incorporates classic Georgian medieval decorative elements. The museum traces its history back to 1852, when the Russian Imperial Geographical Society founded an institution to showcase historically significant items from across the Caucasus.

The first floor of the museum houses a collection of archaeological and ethnographical artefacts from the Neolithic, Bronze, Iron and Middle Ages. The second and third floors are dedicated to the Museum of Soviet Occupation (the main ticket price includes to the exhibit) and give a fascinating insight into this dark period of Georgia's history.

The museum is open from Tuesdays to Sundays from 10 am to 6 pm. The entrance fee is 7 GEL.

Viceroy's (or Vorontsov's) Palace

This palace was one of the very first buildings to have been built on Rustaveli Avenue, dating back to 1807, as the residence of the Russian Viceroy *(Map A, Point 4)*. The arcade, with its many impressive arches, was added later in the middle of the nineteenth century. At one time Stalin's mother lived here, although nowadays it is mainly used for youth activities.

It is often referred to as 'Vorontsov's Palace', honouring one of the more popular Russian Viceroys who oversaw a period of renaissance in Georgia, from 1844 to 1853. During his rule, he embarked upon many initiatives, founding theatres, libraries and museums, and restoring churches and historical monuments. He paid particular attention to education and the preservation of Georgian culture and made the teaching of Georgian compulsory. This commitment to local culture was even more remarkable considering that the official Russian policy was to further its way of life throughout the empire.

However, the history of this building does not end with the retirement of Vorontsov as Viceroy. In 1917, after the Russian Revolution and the collapse of the Russian Empire, the three Caucasian countries, Georgia, Armenia and Azerbaijan, rejected Lenin's new regime. The states instead formed their own Transcaucasian Federation, which met in the Vorontsov Palace throughout 1917. However, Georgians kept insisting on their national independence, and on 26 May 1918, they declared independence, prompting the collapse of the Federation. The Independence Act, which ushered in the first Georgian Republic, was signed here. Armenia and Azerbaijan also declared independence from here in the following days.

Georgian National Parliament

Next door to Vorontsov's Palace, a few steps further up Rustaveli Avenue, is the monumental former Georgian parliament building *(Map A, Point 5)*. Its role as the home to national legislators came to an abrupt end in 2012 when parliament was moved to a futuristic new home in Kutaisi, more than 200 km to the west. However, as all the ministries are still in Tbilisi, many MPs regard this separation as inefficient. So, who knows, maybe one day parliament might move back.

The parliament building was constructed between 1938 and 1953, partly with the help of German prisoners of war, and was initially designed to house the Georgian Soviet. Since independence, the building has witnessed some of the most critical events of recent modern Georgian history. On the 9 April 1989, Soviet Army troops forcibly broke up anti-Soviet demonstrations outside the parliament building, causing a stampede that killed twenty-one people. This event radicalised Georgian opposition to Soviet power. Then, in 1991 during the Georgian Civil War, government opposition fighters attacked the parliament building. Their action damaged the side wings of the structure and eventually forced the then-President Gamsakhurdia to flee to Armenia and then Chechnya, where he led a government-in-exile for the next eighteen months. Finally, in November 2003, the mass protests of the ultimately peaceful Rose Revolution, occurred in the streets around the parliament building, resulting in the peaceful transition of power from President Shevardnadze to President Saakashvili.

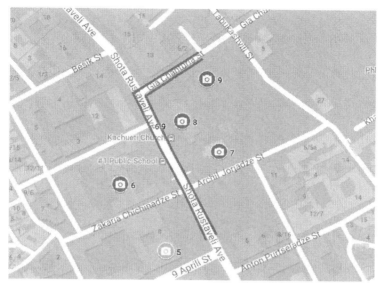

Map B: Georgian National Parliament to 9 April Park

Key:
6. *High School Number 1*
7. *Kashveti Church of St. George*
8. *Georgian National Gallery*
9. *9 April Park*

High School Number 1

The next grand building a few more steps along Rustaveli Avenue is the former High School Number 1, or Classical Gymnasium *(Map B, Point 6)*. This beautiful U-shaped building, surrounding a courtyard planted with mature trees, is a faithful reproduction of the original 1802 structure that was burnt down during the 1991 Georgian Civil War. The

Russian government paid for this reconstruction, and the entire project took a remarkably short two years. During its time as a school, it educated many future leaders who would go on to play key roles in the development of Georgia.

Directly in front of the building are two statues on a single plinth. These are of Ilya Chavchavadze and Akaki Tsereteli, two nineteenth-century Georgian writers who espoused an independent and democratic country.

Chavchavadze is revered today as a national hero, and his fans refer to him as either 'The Uncrowned King' or 'Father of the Nation'. He regarded the three supporting columns of Georgian nationalism as territory, language and Christianity. His death at the hand of assassins galvanised independence movements, culminating in the declaration of independence in 1918.

Akaki Tsereteli, universally known throughout Georgia as just Akaki, was a prolific poet and national liberation movement leader. He published hundreds of patriotic poems, and together with his friend Chavchavadze, spearheaded the independence movement and tirelessly campaigned for a democratic Georgia free of Tsarist interference.

Kashveti Church of Saint George

The Kashveti Church *(Map B, Point 7)* was built quite recently around 1910 but stands on a site that has long held religious significance. In the sixth century, an Assyrian father, Davit Gareja, preached widely throughout Tbilisi and earned the wrath of fire-worshippers who resented his proselytising. According to legend, they bribed a pregnant woman to accuse him of adultery. Upon hearing this, Davit said that if this were indeed true she would give birth to a baby, and if not, a stone. The woman duly gave birth to a stone, and the name Kvashveti derives from this miracle, with 'Kva' meaning stone and 'shva' meaning give birth.

Soon after this occurrence, a church was erected. Hundreds of years later, in 1753, a new sturdier stone structure was built, which was eventually replaced by the church you see today. Its design takes as its inspiration the eleventh-century cathedral of Samtavisi, 60 km northwest of Tbilisi. Inside, the altar was painted by famous Tbilisi artist Ludo Gudiashvili, whose other works are in the Art Museum of Georgia.

Georgian National Gallery

The National Gallery *(Map B, Point 8)* can trace its roots back to the reign of Alexander III, who in the 1880s ordered the construction of a museum dedicated to Russian military history. The museum was intended to show the full glory of the Russian Empire in all of its colonies, something which understandably did not endear it to the locals. It was converted into the National Gallery in 1920 during the shortlived first Democratic Republic of Georgia. It had the broad aim of showcasing 'Georgian, and foreign work from all time periods and artistic movements'.

Today, you can see work from some of Georgia's great painters of the twentieth century, including Gudiashvili and Kakabadze. A highlight is the collection of thirty paintings by Pirosmanashvili who is considered to be one of the greatest artists of the past century, and whose work has been exhibited all around the world. His paintings include portraits of merchants, shopkeepers and workers, and also representations of animals and nature. They are primitivist in style, and do not concern themselves with getting into too much detail; figures often face directly out of the canvas and show little emotion, and some compositions are mainly monochrome. The gallery is open Tuesdays to Sundays from 10 am to 6 pm. The entrance fee is 7 GEL.

Once back on the pavement outside the gallery, look out for a bronze statue depicting a seated lady. The sculpture depicts Elene Akhvlediani, well known for her beautiful paintings of Georgian towns and villages, and for designing theatre sets for major productions in Tbilisi.

9 April Park

After a visit to the National Gallery, you can get a breath of fresh air and enjoy the green spaces of the nearby 9 April Park *(Map B, Point 9)*, which is directly behind the museum. This green space is one of the older parks of Tbilisi and is well known for its big, mature plane trees, which give welcome shade during sunny summer days. It is named to commemorate the sacrifices made by Georgian people during the 1989 anti-Soviet demonstrations.

There are many statues scattered throughout the park, including ones depicting painter Gudiashvili leaning nonchalantly on a lamppost, and Mihaly Zichy, a Hungarian artist well-liked in Georgia for his painting of Shota Rustaveli presenting his poem to Queen Tamar.

Now is a good time to escape the busy city streets and take a side trip up Mount Mtatsminda. To do so, you first need to walk uphill through a quiet and atmospheric neighbourhood of traditional Georgian houses in varying states of repair, and then take a ride to the peak on the Tbilisi Funicular.

From 9 April Park, walk back to Rustaveli Avenue and cross to the other side. Continue up the road for a short distance and turn left up Besik Street. Follow this up the steep hill. Where the street splits, take the left fork and continue up. It eventually becomes Mtatsminda Street. At the junction with Daniel Chonqadze Street, turn left, and the funicular station is on the right.

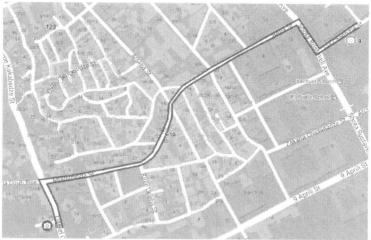

Map C: 9 April Park to Tbilisi Funicular and Mount Mtatsminda sights

Key:
10. Tbilisi Funicular

Tbilisi Funicular

The Tbilisi Funicular *(Map C, Point 10)* dates back all the way to 1905 and aimed to link the remote and undeveloped Mtatsminda plateau with the city 500 m below. When it first opened, the prospect of the cable pulling the carriage snapping terrified the residents to such an extent that they refused to get on board. The owner had to pay the passengers to use the funicular. Once people realised that it was perfectly safe, they queued up to buy tickets, and are still queuing today. So, this funicular has been transporting passengers up to the top of Mount Mtatsminda for well over a century. But don't worry, the operators comprehensively renovated the railway and carriages in 2012.

The lower cable car terminus on Chonqadze Street retains its original turn of the century architecture and resembles something between a fire station and a mosque. The funicular leaves every fifteen to twenty minutes. The cost is 2.5 GEL each way, and you pay with the Tbilisi public transport card; if you don't have one, you can buy one at the lower terminus. Once you leave the station, the journey takes around five minutes. There are spectacular views during the short trip.

The funicular is open daily from 9 am to 4 am.

Mount Mtatsminda

Once you emerge from the funicular carriage and the rather grand collonaded terminal, you are in Mtatsminda Park at the top of the mountain with the same name. The highest point in Tbilisi at a lofty 770 m, you get panoramic views of the entire city of Tbilisi, the surrounding countryside and on clear days the Caucasus mountains around Kazbegi. In the summer, it is also a bit cooler up here, and you can catch some refreshing breezes.

There are a few cafes and restaurants scattered around the area and an amusement park along with a 65 m high outsized Ferris wheel, a roller coaster and various other rides.

In recent years, the park has recently been subject to quite some controversy. It was acquired in the early 2000s by a Georgian billionaire named Badri Patarkatsishvili. However, in 2007, the government of Georgia led by then-president Saakashvili confiscated the businessman's assets, including the park, in response to his political activities which were deemed unwelcome. Patarkatsishvili died the year after, and it was only in 2012 when the government returned his assets to his widow. Saakashvili now faces criminal charges of illegal confiscation, along with many other pending legal actions as a result of his time in office.

Mtatsminda Parthenon and St. Davit's church

Mtstasminda Park also hosts the Georgian National Pantheon, halfway down the slopes of Mount Mtstasminda, in which the most prominent and influential contributors to Georgian culture are interred. These include those whose names you may have already encountered around Tbilisi: the writers and national liberation movement icons Ilia Chavchavadze and Akiko Tsereteli, the poets Giorgi Leonidze and Nikoloz Baratashvili, painter Lado Gudiashvili and theatre director Kote Marjanishvili. Curiously, the mother of Joseph Stalin is also buried here.

Next to the pantheon is the 'Mamadaviti' St. Davit's Church, built in the 1850s over the site of Davit Gareja's medieval cell and chapel. It is from here that the saint would leave his cell to preach the gospel in Tbilisi.

The easiest way to access these sites is to take the funicular down to the middle station. From here it is only a short walk along the hillside.

From the Pantheon, you have two options to get back to Shota Rustaveli Avenue. Firstly, walk down the narrow cobbled street, Mama Davita Rise, back down to its junction with Chonqadze Street. Keep going straight downhill along Mtatsminda street and then Besik Street until you reach the main avenue. Alternatively, retrace your steps back to the funicular station, where you can hop on the next carriage down. Once at the lower terminus, turn left and then take the first right down Mtatsminda Street, following the same route as above. Rustaveli Theatre will be facing you from across the street.

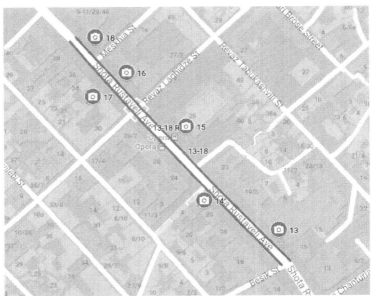

Map D: Rustaveli Theatre to Biltmore Hotel

Key:
13. *Rustaveli Theatre*
14. *Saxophone player sculpture*
15. *Opera and Ballet Theatre*
16. *Zurab Tsereteli Museum of Modern Art*
17. *Prospero's Bookshop*
18. *Biltmore Hotel*

* * *

Rustaveli Theatre

Rustaveli Theatre *(Map D, Point 13)* is one of the oldest and most prominent of Georgia's theatres, built in 1899 in a grand baroque rococo style. Inside, the theatre houses the main auditorium capable of seating more than eight hundred people, and two smaller stages. The famous Georgian painters Gudiashvili and Kakabadze, whose work we saw in the National Gallery, painted frescoes in the basement cafe. However, these were whitewashed over during the Soviet period, and are still undergoing restoration today.

For decades, the director of the theatre was the world-renowned Robert Sturua, famous throughout the art world for his Shakespeare productions. However, he was ignominiously sacked in 2011 after making xenophobic comments about the then-president, implying that a member of the Armenian ethnic minority should not hold such high office. Despite interventions by famous actors, he has not been reinstated.

The theatre's productions are mostly in Georgian, but they occasionally provide English subtitles. There is information on their latest playbill at www.rustavelitheatre.ge.

Saxophone player sculpture

As you walk up the left side of Shota Rustaveli Avenue and approach the junction with Miropan Laghidze Street, keep an eye out for a unique sculpture *(Map D, Point 14)* at number 22. It depicts a saxophone player emerging from the wall, with his torso, one knee and the tips of his shoes poking out from the masonry.

In addition to the saxophonist, many other modern

sculptures adorn the length of this avenue. Many of them depict old Georgian characters, sculpted by the young, self-taught Georgian artist Levan Bujiashvili. There were originally fifty installed, but due to some incidences of theft, forty-two remain. See how many you can spot during your walk!

Opera and Ballet Theatre

Another cultural hotspot of Tbilisi is just 100 m further up the avenue, and the dramatic pseudo-Moorish facade of the Opera and Ballet Theatre *(Map D, Point 15)* is one of the most distinctive in the city.

The theatre has had an unfortunate past and has kept the city's fire brigade busy. The original building opened in 1851 and was one of the many cultural projects undertaken by Governor Vorontsov, yet unfortunately burnt down to the ground in 1874. It was replaced in the 1890s by the magnificent Moorish structure designed by P. Sretter. However, this also burned down in the 1970s, leaving only the front facade, foyer and some side walls. Luckily for us, it was comprehensively reconstructed to preserve its original appearance.

The theatre now stages a packed schedule of opera and ballet throughout the year, and its troupes embark upon extensive international tours. The internationally-successful Georgian tenor Badri Maysuradze currently leads acts as Artistic Director of the theatre, while decorated prima ballerina Nina Ananiashvili heads the ballet troupe. Full programme information, in English, is available on their website at www.opera.ge.

* * *

Zurab Tsereteli Museum of Modern Art (MOMA)

One block further up Rustaveli Avenue on the same side of the street as the Opera and Ballet Theatre is the Museum of Modern Art *(Map D, Point 16)*. It displays many examples of modern Georgian art, almost entirely from Zurab Tsereteli, the Georgian-born painter and sculptor after whom the museum takes its name. He founded MOMA in Tbilisi and made a grant of two thousand works from his private collection.

Tsereteli is the president of the Russian Academy of Arts and acts as a kind of patriarch of the national art scene. He's a fascinating character, little known in the west, but is probably the most commercially successful living artist in Russia. His work rate is prodigious, to say the least, with hundreds of paintings and dozens of over-sized public sculptures standing throughout Russia and around the world.

MOMA Tbilisi spreads over three floors of beautifully lit and spacious galleries. One level exhibits his large, colourful paintings, another his sketches and the last shows artefacts and displays detailing his long life. You can also see some of his sculptures scattered throughout the building.

The museum is open Tuesdays to Sundays from 11 am to 6 pm, and the entrance fee is 5 GEL.

Prospero's Bookshop

Opposite MOMA is a wonderful English language bookshop *(Map D, Point 17)*. Cross the road, and walk through the archway into the hidden internal courtyard. The bookshop has a great selection of titles you would not easily find back home, including translated Georgian fiction, other south

Caucasus novels and a nice range of local travel literature. Maps are also available. This shop is a real find for all bookworms.

You can relax then relax in the courtyard flicking through your new purchases while sipping a coffee from the neighbouring Caliban Coffee Shop.

Prospero's is open daily from 9.30 am to 8 pm.

Biltmore Hotel

Look across the street, and to the left of the MOMA, you will see the Stalinist collonaded facade of a building which was constructed in 1938 to house the Institute of Marxism-Leninism. Its use now couldn't be more different and is safe to say that the two revolutionary leaders will be spinning in their graves. Today, it is the home of the recently-opened five-star Biltmore Hotel *(Map D, Point 18)*, the first to be built outside the United States. The new skyscraper behind this older building, which to some literally sticks out like a sore thumb, was constructed as part of the hotel complex.

The Stalinist structure was originally slated to be almost entirely demolished, leaving behind just one facade. However, a public outcry and protests by preservationists eventually prevented this cultural vandalism from happening.

Continue following Rustaveli Avenue as it curves to the left around the outer fringes of Rose Revolution Square. The next grand building on your left will be the Georgian National Academy of Sciences.

* * *

Tbilisi

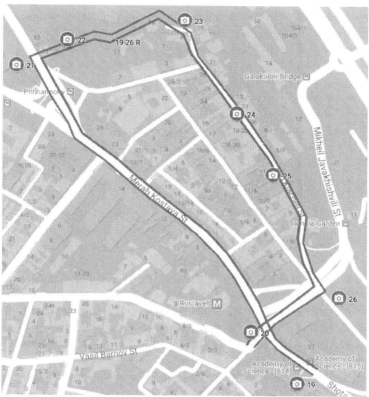

Map E: Academy of Sciences to Rose Revolution Square

Key:
19. *Georgian National Academy of Sciences*
20. *Rustaveli Square*
21. *Tbilisi Concert Hall*
22. *Vera Park*
23. *Lurji Monastery*
24. *Vera Pub Streets*
25. *Elena Akhvledianai Museum*
26. *Rose Revolution Square*

Stephen Stocks

* * *

Georgian National Academy of Sciences

The Georgian National Academy of Sciences *(Map E, Point 19)* was established in 1941 and continues to be the principle learned society of the country. It coordinates scientific research, supervises forty scientific institutes and promotes international collaborations.

The building is another example of classic socialist architecture, built in the 1950s following an architectural competition. The long front of the building faces Rustaveli Avenue while its shorter western section looks out onto Rustaveli Square, and where the two facades meet there is a 55 m tower topped with a metal steeple. Usually, at most times of the day, there are dozens of souvenir sellers in front of the building, with their wares arranged on the steps. It's a good place to pick up a bargain, after a bit of negotiating of course.

Rustaveli Square

Cross Kakabadzeebi Street from the Academy of Sciences and you'll be in the small Rustaveli Square *(Map E, Point 20)*. Here you can find the red line Rustaveli metro station and on a corner the prominent McDonalds restaurant, which was the very first to be opened in Georgia.

Pride of place in the centre of the square is a statue of the great poet Shota Rustaveli himself. He stands on a tall rectangular plinth, at the base of which are reliefs showing scenes from his masterpiece 'The Knight in the Panther's Skin'. This is where the Rustaveli Avenue comes to an end.

Beyond the square, Rustaveli Avenue becomes Kostava Street and enters the trendy Vera district.

Continue to walk straight, along Kostava Street.

Tbilisi Concert Hall

This modern round building *(Map E, Point 21)* plays host to Georgian and international artists and bands. Here the road splits, with Kostava Street passing to the right of the hall. Look to the right, and you will see the entrance to Vera Park.

Vera Park

Vera Park *(Map E, Point 22)* is a beautiful green space at the heart of the Vera district, filled with pine trees and winding pathways. It's a relaxing place to enjoy a snack or drink from one of the stall vendors.

The 1970s late Soviet Modernist building in the centre of the park is the Chess Club, named after the five-time world chess champion, Georgian-born Nona Gaprindashvili. The whole building is planned around a 500-plus seat auditorium which hosts high profile chess games.

Walk to the right of the chess palace to the edge of the park, and you should find some steps leading down to two churches.

Stephen Stocks

Lurji Monastery

'Lurji' in Georgian translates as blue, and this name derives from the glazed blue tiled roof of the church. Dedicated to St. Andrew, it dates from the end of the twelfth century. It has been damaged and renovated many times over, so what you see today is a mix of construction from different periods *(Map E, Point 23)*. Only the lower half of the southern wall, the eastern facade and a few rows of stones within the northern and western walls remain. Extravagant frescoes decorate just about every square inch of the interior.

In the mid-nineteenth century, during Russian rule, the conical Georgian-style dome was replaced with a Russian Orthodox-style onion dome, creating an uneasy hybrid. The offending dome was only restored after independence in 1990. In Soviet times, further indignities were heaped on the church, and it was first used as a sawmill and then as a museum of medicine.

Next to Lurji Monastery is the bigger, onion-domed Russian Orthodox church dedicated to St. John the Theologian. The church was built at the turn of the twentieth century under the orders of then-Governor Golicin. Compared with its more richly decorated neighbour, the interior is mostly simple white and light blue plasterwork. The most colourful spot in the entire church is the golden iconostasis in front of the altar.

Vera 'Pub Streets'

Beginning from just outside Lurji Monastery is Kiacheli Street *(Map E, Point 24)*. Together with its parallel sister Akhvledian (or Petrovskaya) Street, these two narrow streets are lined with pubs and restaurants and are one of the liveliest areas for nightlife in the whole of Tbilisi. It's a great place to come back to in the evening.

From the monastery, remain on Kiacheli Street. Down towards the bottom of the street is the Elena Akhvlediani Museum, on the right-hand side.

Elena Akhvlediani Museum

Elena Akhvlediani, one of the most prominent Georgian artists of the twentieth century, lived much of her life at 12 Kiacheli Street *(Map E, Point 24)*. As you may remember, there is also a statue to Elena Akhvlediani outside the National Gallery. When she died in 1975, she bequeathed her home to the Georgian National Museum so that the public could experience for themselves where she lived and work.

During her time in the house, Akhvlediani hosted many gatherings for Georgia's leading artists and often staged exhibition evenings showing her latest work. The house has a unique and compelling atmosphere built up over the years of her artistic endeavours, and this is still very much evident today. It has a typical Georgian interior, and there are more than three thousand artefacts including paintings, theatrical sketches, illustrations, photos and personal items.

As well as painting life in Georgian towns and villages, Akhvlediani also designed sets for the Marjanishvili Theatre and illustrated the works of national hero and liberation movement leader Ilia Chavchavadze.

Stephen Stocks

Rose Revolution Square

By strolling down to the end of Kiacheli Street, you will emerge into the wide, open expanse of the Rose Revolution Square *(Map E, Point 26)*. This wide open space was built in 1983 and called Republic Square. Its name was later changed to commemorate the 2003 uprising which resulted in the peaceful transition of power.

Protests started when international observers declared that the elections held at the beginning of November 2003 fell short of international standards. The demonstrations lasted for three weeks and reached their peak on 22 November when opposition party supporters burst into the parliament, clutching roses, and forced the then-president Eduard Shevardnadze to flee. Soon after he called for the support of the military, but they refused, prompting him to resign. New presidential and parliamentary elections saw the old Soviet leader replaced by Mikheil Saakashvili.

A short walk to the west of Rose Revolution Square brings you back to Rustaveli Square, where this walking tour ends.

At the Rustaveli Square metro station, you can catch a red line train back to Freedom Square, or if you feel energetic stroll back along Rustaveli Avenue.

PART 2 - Wandering west of the Mtkvari River

Gorgasali Square

Gorgasali Square *(Map F, Point 27)* is the starting point for this walking tour of the neighbourhoods roughly to the west and southwest of the Mtkvari river.

Today, the square is a bustling crossroads, often with queues of traffic honking their horns. Things were not that much different back in the seventeenth and eighteenth centuries when the square was the site of a crowded bazaar attracting traders from Russia, the Middle East and from along the Silk Road. Instead of traffic jams, camel trains would have brought spices, carpets and silk, while Georgians would have sold weapons, wine, metalwork and woollen goods.

From the square, Vakhtang Gorgasali Street heads off south down the river towards Abanotubani (see walking tour 3), and the Metekhi bridge crosses the Mtkvari river to the east bank (see walking tour 4).

This tour will instead go north, plunging deep into the winding alleyways of the old town, starting with Shardeni Street.

* * *

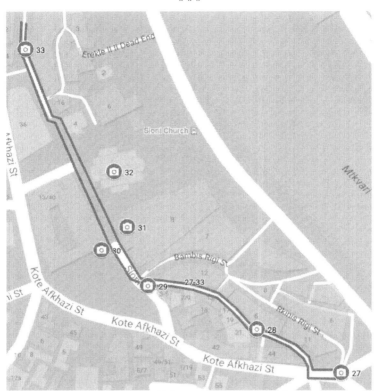

Map F: Gorgasali Square to Erekle II Street

Key:
27. *Gorgasali Square*
28. *Shardeni Street*
29. *Toastmaster Statue*
30. *Hidden bakery*
31. *Tbilisi History Museum*
32. *Sioni Cathedral*
33. *Erekle II Street*

* * *

Shardeni Street

Walk out of the square, away from the river, along Kote Afkhazi Street and take Shardeni Street *(Map F, Point 28)* on the immediate right. This picturesque narrow thoroughfare takes its name from Jan Chardin, the French explorer who visited Tbilisi in the mid-nineteenth century.

You can have a relaxing walk along this pedestrianised street while admiring the grapevine-covered houses. This street is a magnet for tourists, and here you can find every imaginable restaurant and souvenir shop.

Toastmaster statue

Where Shardeni Street meets Sioni Street, you can see the statue of the toastmaster *(Map F, Point 29)*, perched somewhat precariously in the middle of the junction. This sculpture shows a tamada, someone who plays an essential role in Georgian feasts, weddings and other special occasions.

The statue depicts a man about to take a sip from a cow's horn drinking vessel and is modelled on a much earlier figurine from the ancient kingdom of Colchis on the Black Sea coast of modern-day Georgia. Incidentally, Colchis was famous in Greek mythology as the destination of the Argonauts and the home of the Golden Fleece. In Colchian times, the Pagan population worshipped various idols, and foremost among these was the moon, with people often sacrificing bulls in its honour. Bull horns are crescent-shaped and reminiscent of the phase of the moon associated with new life and rejuvenation, and were accordingly used by tamadas at feasts for toasts.

Tamadas were crucial to the success of a gathering and

celebrants chose them with extreme care. Above all, they needed to be eloquent, and indeed some of the best tamadas were accomplished poets and writers. They also needed to organise entertainment well, be aware of sensitivities and politics among the guests, and control the pace of toasting according to the level of inebriation!

Even today you can see horns make an appearance at weddings, and all self-respecting gift shops in Tbilisi have a few for sale among all the other souvenirs.

'Hidden' bakery

From the Toastmaster statue, turn right up Sioni Street. If you are feeling peckish and in the mood for a quick snack, then pay close attention to the building ahead on the left *(Map F, Point 30)*. At its corner, you will see a set of doors from which a staircase descends. Down there in a vaulted basement, you will find a busy bakery, churning out a vast selection of hot Georgian bread and pastries straight from the oven. You shouldn't miss out on this culinary treat, but if you have difficulty finding it ask a local and they will know how to get there for sure.

Tbilisi History Museum

Continuing up Sioni Street, and you'll find the Tbilisi History Museum *(Map F, Point 31)* after a few short steps. This institution is in a restored three-storey caravanserai, which used to provide accommodation to weary travellers on the old Silk Road.

The museum's permanent exhibition displays artefacts

from prehistory up to the present day, with an emphasis on the last two centuries. On the ground floor, several shops offer for sale local art, pottery and jewellery.

The museum is open daily from 10 am to 6 pm, except Mondays.

Sioni Cathedral of the Dormition

The compact Sioni Cathedral *(Map F, Point 32)*, right next to the Tbilisi History Museum, is one of the landmarks of Tbilisi's old quarter. It takes its name from the Zion hill in Jerusalem which is the location of the city of David.

King Vakhtang Gorgasali ordered the construction of the church way back in the fifth century, yet building work only began one hundred years later in 575. They completed its construction in the early seventh century. However, the structure you see today is not the medieval original, thanks to the particularly turbulent and violent Georgian history, and the first church was destroyed by invading Arabs. King David IV, one of the greatest and most successful rulers of Georgia, rebuilt the church, and the fundamental parts of today's structure date from then. Subsequent conquests by Timur, and later the Persians, saw extensive restorations in the fifteenth and seventeenth centuries, and a major earthquake in 1668 prompted further renovations.

The church is made from a yellowish volcanic rock called tuff, quarried from an area to the southwest of Tbilisi, and is an archetypal example of medieval Georgian church architecture. The cross-shaped plan of the structure is much squarer than churches in western Europe. At the centre of the cross is a tall drum topped with a conical dome. You'll see this church design throughout Tbilisi and at some of the famous hilltop sites such as Gergeti.

While the exterior of Sioni Cathedral is mostly without any ornamentation, dazzling frescoes cover the inside. Those in the dome and upper parts of the cathedral date from the 1840-50s and were painted by the Russian nobleman and military administrator, Prince Grigory Gagarin. The lower frescoes are quite modern, painted in 1989 by Georgian artist Levan Tsutskiridze.

The highlight of the cathedral and the reason for its unique significance for Georgians is the grapevine cross of Saint Nino, a major symbol of the Georgian Orthodox Church. Saint Nino purportedly received this directly from the Virgin Mary, and then secured it by entwining her hair. She introduced Christianity to Georgia and carried the cross, which is particularly distinctive due to its drooping arms, on her evangelical mission. Throughout its long history, it has been hidden at many locations to protect it from invading armies, and it has resided at the Sioni Cathedral since 1802. The one you see is a replica; the original is kept safe somewhere deep within the cathedral. Also inside are the tombs of many Catholicos-Patriarchs, the heads of the Georgian Orthodox Church.

Outside again, to the north of the cathedral, you'll see a freestanding three-storey belfry. King Alexander the First built this bell tower during one of the main reconstructions, this time repairing the damage wrought by invading Timurid forces. Don't confuse this with another three-storey bell tower across the street; that one was built in 1812 to commemorate Russian victory over the Ottoman empire.

Erekle II Street

Continuing north from Sioni Cathedral, Sioni Street becomes Erekle II Street *(Map F, Point 33)* after a few metres. This street, entirely lined with bars and restaurants, is named after Heraclius II. This king, also known as Erekle II, reigned over the Georgian regions of Kartli and Kakheti in the latter half of the eighteenth centuries.

The rows of bars and cafes come to an end at the junction of Antimoz Ivereli Lane. Turn right here for a brief detour to see the Bridge of Peace.

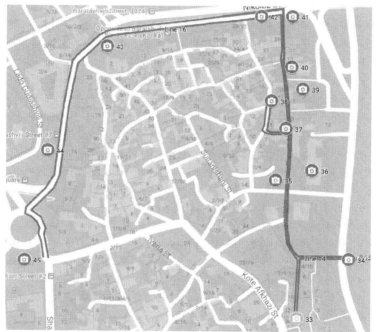

Map G: Erekle II Street to Tbilisi Town Hall

Key:
  34. *Bridge of Peace*
  35. *Erekles Square*
  36. *Patriarchate of Georgia*

Bridge of Peace

This striking 150-metre long pedestrian bridge *(Map G, Point 34)* spanning the Mtkvari river is a relatively new addition to the Tbilisi cityscape, completed in 2010. It was commissioned to connect the old town on the west bank with the new quarters over on the east. The architects built the entire bridge in Italy in various modules, transported them across Europe in two hundred trucks and then assembled the structure on site.

The bridge is unreservedly modernist, constructed from steel with a curving glass canopy. At night, the thousands of embedded LED lights within its structure come to life, producing a shimmering light display. It communicates, in Morse code, the chemical elements found in the human body. The intention is to celebrate life and peace between people by telling the story of what makes up each one of us.

Such an incongruous feature placed next to the old town has attracted its fair share of criticism, although it seems to be a firm favourite with visitors and a popular selfie spot. As you walk to the centre of the bridge, you can enjoy panoramic views of pretty much all the significant landmarks of Tbilisi, including Metekhi Church, the Vakhtang Gorgasali statue, Narikala fortress, Rike Park and the Presidential Palace.

* * *

Retrace your steps back along the bridge to where you began, then turn right to continue along Erekles II Street.

Erekles Square

Further ahead you come to Erekles Square *(Map G, Point 35)*, a leafy park with cobbled walkways which until the mid-nineteenth century was the famous central square of the whole of Tbilisi. It was also known as Batoni's (Lord's) Square because the palace of King Rustam stood on this spot until invading Persian forces ruined it in 1795.

On the northern edge of the square, you will see the ornate balconies of the palace of King Giorgi XII, the last king of Georgia. His reign was shortlived, beginning in 1798 and ending with his death in 1800, at which point Georgia became part of the Russian Empire.

From Erekles Square, Erekle II Street becomes the narrow Ione Shavteli Street, the commercial heart of the old city in medieval times.

Patriarchate of Georgia

Across the street from Erekles Square is the imposing bulk of the Patriarchate of Georgia *(Map G, Point 36)*, built on the site of the destroyed palace of King Rustam. Initially intended as a governor's residence and administrative block, religious authorities procured the building in 1848, and it has had an ecclesiastical use ever since. Today it houses the headquarters of the Georgian Orthodox Church.

This religion plays a dominant role in Georgian life,

counting more than 84% of the population as followers. It has been the state religion for pretty much all of the sixteen or so centuries since its introduction by Saint Nino, except during the Soviet years, and is considered to be the country's most influential institution. It is currently headed by Catholicos-Patriarch Ilia II, who has held the position for more than forty years.

Kari Saint George Church

Just to the northern of Erekles Square is the diminutive Kari church *(Map G, Point 37)*. A much older church built by Vakhtang Gorgasali (who also ordered the construction of Sioni Cathedral) originally stood on this site. With much else, it was destroyed by the Mongols in their late fourteenth-century rampage through the city. Eventually, in the 1640s, three new churches were built here using the rubble from the original structure, dedicated to Saint John, the Annunciation, and Saint George, with only the last surviving today. For much of its life the church has operated as the court church, hence its name 'Kari'.

Nikoloz Baratashvili Memorial House

Walk down the small alleyway running past the church, away from Shavteli Street, and then right onto Chakhrukhadze Street. Number seventeen on the right-hand side is the house in which the Georgian romantic poet Nikoloz Baratashvili lived, now a memorial museum *(Map G, Point 38)*. In this part of town, you will also see a major road and bridge named after him and on the other bank of the river a prominent statue.

Baratashvili is a giant of Georgian literature, and spearheaded the development of nineteenth-century Georgian literature and introducing 'Europeanism'. He died when he was only twenty-six, and so his works only comprise forty short lyrics, a longer poem and some private letters. Nonetheless, fans sometimes refer to him as Georgia's Byron.

The museum displays many different artefacts related to the great poet's life, including furniture, folk musical instruments, paintings, manuscripts and books. As 2017 marked the two hundredth anniversary of his birth, the Tbilisi museum authority undertook a comprehensive renovation and introduced 3D animation holograms and multimedia displays to tell the story of Baratashvili.

Anchiskhati Basilica

Retrace your steps back down Chakhrukhadze Street, turn left and then left again and you'll find yourself back on Shatvali Street. After a few short steps, you will come across one of the old town's highlights, and longest surviving church, the sixth-century Anchiskhati Basilica *(Map G, Point 39)*. It was purportedly built by King Dachi of Iberia when he made Tbilisi his capital.

The church was originally dedicated to the Virgin Mary. However, its name was changed in 1675 when the precious twelfth-century icon of the Saviour was moved there from the remote Ancha monastery to prevent it falling into the hands of Ottoman marauders (Anchiskhati means 'icon of Ancha).

As with many churches and important buildings in Tbilisi, the basilica has been through the wars a bit and accordingly has had a few renovations and reconstructions. In the seventeenth century, some parts of the upper church and the bell tower were rebuilt in brick, and in the 1870s a dome was added. The oldest and most original parts of the church are the walls, constructed from the same yellow tuff material used in for the Sioni Cathedral.

The interior is dark and mysterious, lightened somewhat by the many devotional candles. Most of the paintings date from the nineteenth century, except for those in the altar screen which were commissioned by the then Catholicos-Patriarch of Georgia, Nikoloz Amilakhvari.

The church was closed down during the Soviet era and converted to a museum of handicrafts. However, following independence, it resumed its central role in the religious life of Georgia. It is home to the Anchiskhati choir, which is known throughout choral circles globally as one of the best performers of Georgian polyphonic choral music.

Around the embankment side of the church, you will see a sculpture showing the head of Nodar Dumbadze, one of the most popular Georgian writers of the last century. Most of his novels have since been made into films. His early books, such as Granny, Iliko, Illarion and I (1960) and I See the Sun (1962) are semi-autobiographical and gives a fascinating insight into Georgian village life during World War Two.

Rezo Gabriadze Puppet Theatre and Clock Tower

Back on Shatvali Street, continue north, and you will come across an apparently ancient and slightly ramshackle clock tower *(Map G, Point 40)*, which looks as if it has been plucked directly from the pages of a fairy tale. However, don't let appearances deceive you. The tower was erected only in 2010 by the renowned Georgian artist, writer and director Rezo Gabriadze. He designed the tower himself, using a mix of medieval architectural features so that it blends harmoniously with the surrounding old town. At the top of every hour, an angel comes out of the tower to ring the bell with her hammer, so if you are walking past at this time make sure you stop to watch.

The puppet theatre itself, while modest in size, is well-regarded internationally as a preeminent cultural institution, with high-quality marionette performances. The theatre also makes extensive tours and has brought its show to New York, London, Edinburgh, Toronto and Moscow among other far-flung venues.

The original and particularly moving plays comprising the repertoire of the theatre were all written by Gabriadze, and include *Stalingrad*, a requiem for the great battle, and *The Autumn of My Spring* which tells the story of life in impoverished post-war Georgia.

Gabriadze is also famous for the films that he has written, including *Don't Grieve*, *Mimino* and *Kin-Dza-Dza*. His characters from Mimino are immortalised in the sculpture nearby the Avlabari metro station on the other side of the Mtkvari river.

You should book in advance as performances tend to fill up quickly.

Berikaoba sculpture

At the end of Shatveli Street, on the corner at the junction with Baratashvili is the Berikaoba sculpture *(Map G, Point 41)*, showing an old Pagan festival where actors parade childishly and playfully through village streets.

The principal characters are a bride and a groom, accompanied by several men (berika) disguised as common Georgian animals such as the wolf, bear and boar. Their wedding is broken up by marauding Tatars, who proceed to kill the groom and kidnap the bride. The berika eventually resuscitate the groom with healing water and minerals, who then goes on to chase the Tatars and rescue the bride. The performance ends with a lavish Georgian feast, the supra.

The festival is held around the time of the spring equinox and celebrates the rebirth of nature. It aims to ensure a fertile and fruitful agricultural year ahead.

The sculpture exudes joy and cheerfulness and brings out the playful nature of the Berikaoba festival. Passers-by are free to enter the circle and pose with the statues any way they see fit and is a great photo opportunity!

Baratashvili Street

Walking from the Berikaoba statue, away from the river along Baratashvili Street *(Map G, Point 42)*, you will start to see remains of the old Tbilisi walls. The division between the older and newer parts of the city is apparent here. On the right-hand side of the street are the relatively modern blocks constructed in the 1950s and 1960s. The street plan extending outwards from that side is more regular and grid-like. On the left side, there are the old eighteenth-century city walls topped by handsome balconied buildings. Many of these now function as restaurants. These walls were uncovered in the 1970s when existing buildings were demolished when Georgian architect Shota Kavlashvili redeveloped this part of the city. There is a statue to this architect at the end of this stretch of wall.

Tbilisi

Ancient city walls

Further along, Baratashvili Street becomes Pushkin Street. At this point, the remains of twelfth and thirteenth-century walls *(Map G, Point 43)* were discovered when Pushkin Street was renovated in 2012. Many fragments of twelfth-century glazed pottery were also found. The municipality built bridges to protect all this archaeology, and today the road and pavements pass safely overhead. Pedestrian walkways were also made under the bridges so that visitors can view the walls up close.

The remains included several towers, and you can see multiple layers showing that they had repeatedly been destroyed by invaders and then subsequently rebuilt with different materials. The last destruction of the walls was in 1801 when the Russian Empire annexed Georgia. Roads and buildings were built on top of the ruins in the intervening years, and the walls were forgotten until their recent unearthing.

Pushkin Park

Pushkin Street, named after the famous Russian poet and author, eventually leads you to Pushkin Park *(Map G, Point 44)* on the left, also named after the great man. This pretty little green space is an extension of Freedom Square.

As well as a statue of Pushkin, the park also contains the grave of Kamo, a Bolshevik revolutionary and early confidante of Stalin, whose real name was Simon Petrosian. Kamo carried out many militant operations in Georgia in the first few years of the twentieth century. The most dramatic of these was the robbing of vast sums of money from a bank in

Freedom Square. Kamo personally delivered the cash to Lenin to help fund further revolutionary activities. He came to a sticky end in 1922 when he was run over by a truck while cycling in Tbilisi, widely believed to have been the work of assassins under Stalin's orders. It is ironic that his grave is in full view of the bank that he robbed years earlier. The monument has since been removed, but the grave itself, now unmarked, is somewhere between the fountain and Pushkin's statue.

Tbilisi Town Hall

Across Freedom Square is the Tbilisi Town Hall *(Map G, Point 45)*, with its impressive facade and clock tower topped by the fluttering Georgian flag. This building contains the mayor's office and the City Assembly. Most of the departments managing the city, such as transport, educations, welfare and urban planning, are housed within its walls.

The town hall was built during Russian rule in the 1830s but has since experienced many renovations and reconstructions. The present facade is the result of an ambitious redesign by architect Paul Stern in the neo-Moorish style that was all the rage at that time. The clock tower is even more modern, added in 1912.

As you face the Town Hall, walk down Kote Afghazi street leaving Freedom Square on your left. Continue straight then turn right down Abesadze Street. Then after 200 m or so turn left onto Anton Katalikos Street.

* * *

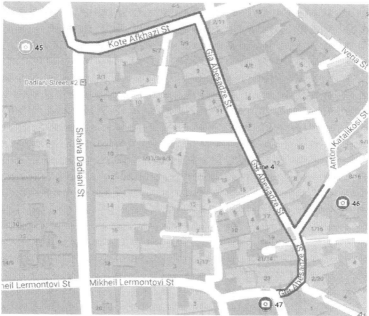

Map H: Tbilisi Town Hall to Lado Gudiashvili Square

Key:
   45. *Tbilisi Town Hall*
   46. *David Baazov Museum of the History of the Jews*
   47. *Lado Gudiashvili Square*

David Baazov Museum of the History of the Jews

The David Baazov Museum *(Map H, Point 46)* is at 3 Anton Katalikos Street, housed in a distinctive, red-brick, dome-shaped former synagogue. It was established in 1933 to tell the centuries-long history of Jewish life in Georgia, and to study Jewish-Georgian relations. This quite small but never fascinating museum displays interesting artefacts such as Torahs, menorah candelabra, religious clothing, paintings, photographs and other documents.

The Jewish community in Georgia is one of the oldest in the country, with the first migration occurring in the sixth century BC following the Babylonian siege of Jerusalem. Since then, up until Soviet times, the Jews and other Georgians lived harmoniously with an almost total lack of anti-Semitism. The USSR, however, terminated Zionist activity in the country, and the Jewish community's situation only improved in the 1990s when Georgia obtained its independence.

David Baazov was a Georgian-born Jew who became a prominent rabbi at the turn of the century. He organised an all-Jewish Congress in Tbilisi at the end of World War I, which brought together delegations from every Jewish community in the country. He also established Jewish schools across Georgia, founded a Jewish newspaper and organised migration to Israel following a Soviet crackdown on Jewish institutions. In Stalin's 1938 purge, he was arrested and exiled to Siberia. He returned to Georgia in 1945 but died soon after that.

The museum is open daily from 11 am to 5 pm.

From the museum, retrace your steps along Anton Katalikos Street and then turn left onto Abesadze Street. Continue until you reach Lado Gudiashvili Square.

Lado Gudiashvili Square

The quaint, cobbled Lado Gudiashvili Square *(Map H, Point 47)*, is named after the twentieth-century painter and famous son of Tbilisi. His paintings had strong mythological and poetic themes and are seen to combine the traditions of Georgian art with that of French symbolism. Some of Gudiashvili's works hang in the Art Museum of Georgia.

Crumbling nineteenth and early twentieth century buildings, replete with distinctive wrought-iron balconies surround the square on all sides. These are original facades, and minimal restoration has been done over the past century, giving the area an unforgettable atmosphere.

However, recent urban development policies have thrust the area into controversy. In 2011, the plans of an Austrian consortium prompted the establishment by residents of an 'Occupy Gudiashvili' movement to stop what they saw as cultural vandalism. The action generated considerable media coverage, and the plans were eventually shelved. At the time of writing, in 2018, the mayor has officially kicked off a more sympathetic renovation project which aims to fully restore eighteen prominent buildings and preserve the area's cultural heritage.

Walk down the western edge of the square and exit on Beglar Akhospireli Street. After 100 m you will reach Asatiani Street. Cross the street and continue straight along Betlemi Rise.

Stephen Stocks

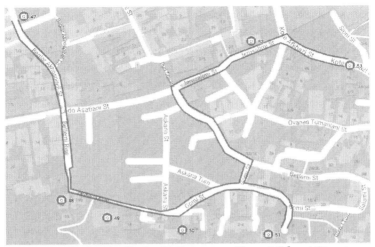

Map I: Lado Gudiashvili Square to Kote Afkhazi Street

Key:
47. *Lado Gudiashvili Square*
48. *Lower Betlemi Church*
49. *Upper Betlemi Church*
50. *Ateshgah Fire Temple*
51. *Kldisubani St. Geroge Church*
52. *Jvaris Mama and Noroshen Churches*
53. *Kote Afkhazi Street*

Betlemi Neighbourhood

This district is one of the oldest in the whole of Tbilisi and nestles against the slopes which lead up to the Narikala fortress. It traces its history back to the very founding of Tbilisi, and the winding layout of the streets is evidence of this neighbourhood's long past. Most of the houses you see are built over the remains, or incorporate parts, from much older predecessors.

This area is built on a series of terraces connected by narrow lanes and street stairs. Its a maze of balconied old houses, churches and courtyards. Yes, it is damaged, faded and non-maintained, but this only adds to its beauty and atmosphere.

Lower Betlemi Church

The first church you encounter on the right is Lower Betlemi *(Map I, Point 48)*. This site originally had a nunnery and a small chapel, built by Armenians emigrating from Iran in the early eighteenth century. The current structure was built in 1868 and continued to be used as an Armenian place of worship right up until 1988 when it was handed over to the Georgian Orthodox Church. In the intervening years, it has been 'Georganised', with the removal of specific inscriptions and architectural features, and the addition of new Georgian frescoes.

Upper Betlemi Church

A few more steps along Betlemi Rise you come across Upper Betlemi Church *(Map I, Point 49)*. Legend has it that the original church on this site was built by King Vakhtang Gorgali way back in the sixth century. Whatever the veracity of this very early history, we know that the Armenians established the Virgin Mary Church here in the fifteenth century, which was replaced by the construction of the current church in 1740.

* * *

Stephen Stocks

Ateshgah Fire Temple

Continue walking along Betlemi Rise to its junction with Gomi Street, where you will find the remains of a fifth-century Zoroastrian fire temple *(Map I, Point 50)*. To get up close to the Ateshgah is rather tricky, and you will need to weave through the courtyards of the neighbourhood to get there.

Ateshgah resembles an old cube made from red brick. It is thought to have been built during the time of the Persian Sasanid empire, and the name 'Ateshgah' means 'the place for fire' in Persian. It is one of the very oldest structures in Tbilisi.

Zoroastrianism has the distinction of being the world's first monotheistic religion and takes its name from its founder, the Persian prophet Zoroaster. Adherents to the faith worshiped a god called Ahura Mazda, and fire was the most important symbol of the religion as it was considered to represent his holy spirit. For centuries Zoroastrianism was the dominant religion of Persia, and once Georgia came under the influence of the Persian empire, the belief was introduced into the country. While Georgia was already practising Christianity at the time, chroniclers indicate that King Vakhtang Gorgasali was willing to tolerate this new religion. Today, the temple is the only one remaining.

The history of Ateshgah is murky, but sometime during the Ottoman-Persian wars of the eighteenth century, when the Turks seized Tbilisi, the temple was turned into a mosque for a time. In the years after that, Armenian families used it as an accommodation block, and residents remember people living there as recently as the 1970s.

* * *

Tbilisi

Kldisubani St. George Church

Retrace your steps to Gomi street and continue along, with the hillside to your right. Turn down the third alley on you right, Jvaredini Turn, at the end of which is the Kldisubani St. George Church *(Map I, Point 51)*, built right up against the cliff. As with almost all of the churches in this part of town, it is on the site of a much earlier structure dating from the reign of King Vakhtang Gorgasali in the fifth century.

The current structure was built in 1753, paid for by Armenian merchant Petros Zohrabian, and then served the Armenian Christian community. In the Soviet times when religious activities were restricted, the church fell into disuse and was used to make toys. People also built small dwellings in the churchyard. After the fall of the USSR, the Georgian Orthodox authorities appropriated the church, removed all Armenian traces and restored the churchyard to its original state.

Retrace your steps back along Gomi Street. Turn right down a short lane which leads to Betlemi Street. Turn left and keep going until the junction with Asatiani Street. Turn right and keep going until you see Jvaris Mama on the left.

Jvaris Mama and Noroshen Churches

On the corner of Jerusalem Street and the main Kote Afkhazi Street is a compound containing two little churches. The smaller one is Jvaris Mama *(Map I, Point 52)*, which has an incredibly long history going back to the fifth century. This church was built in the sixteenth century and substantially renovated in 1825. The real highlight is the interior, where spectacular red, blue and gold frescoes, just recently restored, cover every square inch.

Also in the same courtyard is the slightly larger Noroshen church, built in 1793, which is undergoing renovation.

Kote Afkhazi Street

The main road running outside Jvaris Mama is Kote Afkhazi Street *(Map I, Point 53)*, ground-zero of all tourist related commerce in Tbilisi. Here you will find a bewildering array of cafes, bars, restaurants, souvenir shops, tour companies and taxi drivers, all competing for your business.

The street takes its name from the prominent early twentieth-century military officer and politician. Kote Afkhazi was a Georgian nobleman who served as a general in Georgia's national army. When the Soviets invaded, he was one of the leading players of an underground anti-Soviet resistance and led many guerilla operations. Eventually, in 1923, the Soviets caught up with him and sentenced him to death. At his execution, he reportedly said: 'I am dying with joy because I'm given the honour to be sacrificed for Georgia.' And so his reputation as a national hero was cemented.

Gorgasali Square

Kote Afkhazi Street leads back to Gorgasali Square, which marks the end point of this route. There are lots of pleasant cafes, restaurants and bars in this area where you can rest your weary feet before starting another walking tour of Tbilisi.

PART 3 - Stepping south from Gorgasali Square

This walking tour steps south of Gorgasali Square to experience sulphur baths, hidden waterfalls and the lofty battlements of Narikala Fortress.

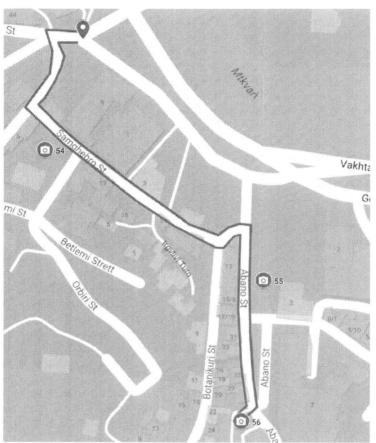

Map J: Gorgasali Square to Orbeliani Baths

Key:
  54. *St. George Armenian Cathedral of Tbilisi*
  55. *Abanotubani Sulphur Baths*
  56. *Orbeliani Baths*

St. George Armenian Cathedral of Tbilisi

From Gorgasali Square, head directly south down Dzmebi Zdanevichebi Street and then take the first left along Samghebro Street. A few steps long you will see the gateway into the compound of the St. George Armenian Cathedral *(Map J, Point 54)*, which stands on a raised platform overlooking Gorgasali Square. It is one of only two still-functioning Armenian churches in Tbilisi, the other being the Ejmiatzin church on the other side of the river in the Avlabari neighbourhood. The religious authorities have since consecrated all the rest as Georgian Orthodox churches.

Among Tbilisi residents, the church is known more popularly as Tsikhisdidi, because it was built on land belonging to the prison. 'Tsikhe' in Georgian means 'prison' and 'didi' translated as 'big'. Some academics believe that the original church was built in 1251 by the wealthy Armenian merchant Umek, and as evidence point to an inscription above the Western door referring to the thirteenth century. However, the Armenian church disputes this theory and suggest instead that churches have stood on this site since 631, and that Umek 'rebuilt' rather than 'built' the church.

The cathedral has had a turbulent history and was burnt by the Persians during their 1795 invasion. As a result, most of the structure you see today dates from the eighteenth and nineteenth centuries. Inside, the frescoes mainly date from the eighteenth century, except for four large murals which were added more recently in 1923. Also look out for the tomb of Saytnova, the renowned eighteenth-century musician and artist, next to the main door.

Stephen Stocks

Abanotubani Sulphur Baths

After walking back out of the cathedral, turn right and continue walking down Samghebro Street. At the end, cross over Botanikuri Street, and you'll be on Abano Street, which marks the beginning of the Abanotubani district where you can find most of Tbilisi's sulphur baths *(Map J, Point 55)*. Your nose will probably detect the rotten egg odour of the sulphur before you catch sight of the baths themselves.

Some say that it was the sulphur springs which bubble up naturally in this area which prompted King Vakhtang Gorgasali to settle here and establish Tbilisi as his capital city. In fact, the 'Tbili' part of the name roughly translates as 'warm' in Georgian. At the peak of their popularity, there were more than sixty sulphur bathhouses here, used by people to cure a variety of medical ailments and aches and pains. Today, five bathhouses remain.

Many famous travellers have enjoyed the pleasures of the baths over the years. The Russian poet Pushkin went so far as to say 'Not since my birth have I witnessed such luxuriousness as at Tbilisi baths'. French author Alexander Dumas waxed even more lyrical, asking 'Why doesn't Paris, the city of physical pleasures, have such baths?'

Directly facing you on Abano Street you see the archetypal red brick domes which cover most of the baths in this area, and in this case these are the domes of the partially subterranean Royal Bathhouse. It's a great spot for photography, with the Narikala fortress and balconied Georgian houses forming a unique backdrop to the bathhouse domes. Another popular bathhouse right next door is Gulo's Thermal Spa. Walk around this compact area, and you will find all the bathhouses and can compare prices for the usual services such as body scrubs, saunas and massages.

Continue to walk up Abano Street, and you will find the

most beautifully ornate baths on the right-hand side. These are the Orbeliani Baths *(Map J, Point 56)*, known colloquially around Tbilisi as the Blue Bathhouse, due to its magnificent blue tiled facade, designed in the style of a Persian mosque. It even has two little minarets.

As you face the Orbeliani Baths, look to your left, and you will see a narrow wooden bridge spanning the small river. Cross this and turn right along the opposite bank.

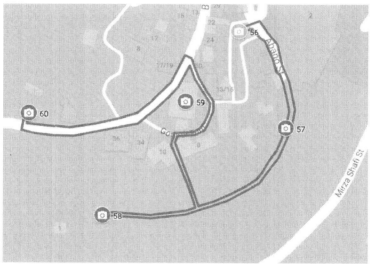

Map K: Orbeliani Baths to the Botanical Gardens

Key:
  56. *Orbeliani Baths*
  57. *Leghvtakhevi*
  58. *Dvzeli Waterfall*
  59. *Jumah Mosque*
  60. *Botanical Gardens*

* * *

Stephen Stocks

Leghvtakhevi and Dvzeli Waterfall

The small stream flowing down the centre of the narrow gorge and past all the bathhouses is the Tsavkisistskali river. Its name means 'waters of Tsavkisi' in English, and indeed the river flows through the small town of Tsavkisi west of Tbilisi. As the river flows down through this gorge and into the Mtkvari, it mingles with the waters emanating from the various sulphur springs, so the smell of rotten eggs pervades here.

As you walk up the river, the gorge narrows and deepens, and the rocky cliffs become higher and higher. Look up, and you will see balconies, and the actual old Georgian houses themselves, protruding precariously over the drop.

This gorge is called Leghvtakhevi *(Map K, Point 57)*, roughly translated as 'gorge of figs' in English, as fig trees used to be common in this area. It has only recently become accessible as a tourist attraction. Before a development project in 2012 the place was quite wild and challenging to get into; since then various walkways, bridges, kiosks and cafes have been opened, and the popularity of the area has soared with visitors and locals alike.

The path meanders along the gorge, occasionally crossing the river over small bridges. Eventually, where the cliffs are at their highest, you reach the dead end of the gorge, over which the Tsavkisistskali river tumbles in a dramatic and unexpected waterfall *(Map K, Point 58)*. It's a real hidden oasis in the middle of the city, that's nice to visit in any season. In summer, the towering cliffs and thundering waterfall cool you down, and in the winter the falls sometimes freeze into a surreal ice sculpture.

Retrace your steps back along the river away from the waterfall.
After a short while, you will see a small arched stone bridge,

overlooked by the multi-coloured balconies of old houses on the top of the cliff. At this point, you should climb the black wrought iron spiral staircase linking the river with the top of the cliff. A few steps through the meandering alleyways will bring you out next to the Jumah mosque.

Jumah Mosque

Tbilisi has long been a melting pot, and this extends to religion. While Georgia is overwhelmingly Orthodox Christian, there has been a remarkable tolerance of other faiths, and the Jumah mosque *(Map K, Point 59)* is on the same road as a church and a synagogue. Muslims currently constitute ten percent of the Georgian population.

The original mosque on this site dates from the 1700s, but as with many other such buildings has been victim to Tbilisi's turbulent history, and has been destroyed and rebuilt three times. The current red-brick mosque was built in 1895. It has a distinct octagonal minaret with a unique Georgian-style balcony at the top.

Unusually, Shia and Sunni Muslims pray side-by-side here, and this is due to the Soviet period of occupation. There were initially two mosques, the Jumah and the Blue mosques, where each sect prayed separately. However, in 1951, the Soviets demolished the Blue mosque to build a bridge, and as the Shias had nowhere to go. The Jumah mosque welcomed them to worship there. At first, a black curtain separated the Shias and Sunnis, but today there is no such division.

Non-Muslim visitors are welcome to go inside while adhering to the usual dress requirements and removal of shoes. The serene interior has some beautiful tiling and frescoes painted in a series of cool blues and greens.

* * *

Stephen Stocks

Botanical Gardens

From the mosque, walk 100 m uphill on Botanikuri Street to reach the entrance to the National Botanical Gardens of Tbilisi *(Map K, Point 60)*. This parkland extends to just under 100 hectares and comprises 4,500 species of plant from the Caucasus and further afield. There is even a Japanese garden

There has long been some form of botanical garden in this part of Tbilisi, and records show that the predecessor of the current garden was in the lower part of the Tsavkisistskali gorge. However, Persian invaders pillaged the original garden in 1795. It was subsequently revived at today's location, with the garden receiving its formal status of National Botanical Garden in 1845.

The most popular time to visit the park is in the spring and summer when the plants are at their best. Due to the garden's size, it is best to wear comfortable walking shoes, particularly as some of the paths and trails are quite rough, and the terrain is hilly.

The next stop on this walking tour is the Narikala Fortress. There are two ways to get there.

***Option 1**: After exploring the National Botanical Gardens, go back to the main entrance on Botanikuri Street. Turn up Orbiri Street on your left, which will meander up the hillside all the way up to the fortress.*

***Option 2**: Within the Gardens themselves there is a path that leads up the ridge and emerges at the Kartlis Deda statue just to the west of the Fortress. However, this can be tricky to find, and signage is limited.*

* * *

Tbilisi

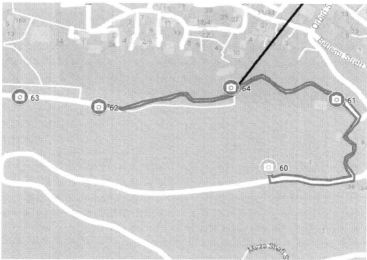

Map L: Botanical Gardens to Aerial Tram and Rike Park

Key:
>   *60. Botanical Gardens*
>   *61. Narikala Fortress*
>   *62. Kartlis Deda*
>   *63. Shahtakhti Fortress and Ivanishvili Residence*
>   *64. Aerial Tram to Rike Park*

Narikala Fortress

Arrayed along the crest of the Solokai ridge, dominating the old town, is the Narikala Fortress *(Map L, Point 61)*, undoubtedly one of the most prominent of all Tbilisi's landmarks. Its strategic importance is apparent when you look at the city under you; the citadel has a panoramic view of the narrowest point of the Mtkvari river and guarded against any attack from the south. Its name means 'impregnable fortress' in English. Remarkably, it dates back more than 1700 years and as you'd expect has witnessed a long and sometimes bloody history.

The Persians laid the initial foundations for the castle in the late fourth century. When King Vakhtang Gorgasali moved his capital to Tbilisi in the next century, he immediately recognised the importance of the Persian fortifications, and he set about enlarging and strengthening them. The next set of occupiers, the Arabs, continued this theme of continually improving the defences, and almost all of the ruined walls you see today are the result of their labours. In the centuries after that, waves of invaders, including Mongolians, Turks and Persians, all left their mark on the structure.

If you are approaching from Orbiri Street, you will first meet a small square tower, through which there is a roughly-hewn gateway. At the top of the steep cobbled path, you will enter the lower court of the fortress, at the centre of which is the St. Nicholas church. While taking the form of a traditional 'inscribed' cross design, this is pretty much brand new, having been built in 1996-7 to replace the destroyed thirteenth-century original. From here you can then explore the battlements of the fortress west along the ridge. Some of the walls have been extensively restored, such as those surrounding St. Nicholas Church, whereas others have been untouched for centuries.

Kartlis Deda

Eventually, you will pass the cable car station, and about 200 m further on is the imposing and somewhat space-age Kartlis Deda (*Map L, Point 62*), or Mother of Georgia statue. This 20 m high woman is designed to represent the Georgian character. She holds a sword in one hand, demonstrating the Georgian's passionate defence of their homeland over the centuries; in the other, she offers a bowl of wine, showing the country's hospitable and welcoming nature. Leading Georgian sculptor Elguja Amashukeli designed the statue, which was erected in 1958 when the city celebrated its 1500th anniversary. Kartlis Deda is now undoubtedly Georgia's most recognised woman and has become a national symbol.

Shahtakhti Fortress and Ivanishvili Residence

Moving past Mother Georgia are the ruins of the Shahtakhti Fortress *(Map L, Point 63)*, which was used as an observatory by the Arabs in the seventh to ninth centuries. Finally, at the extreme western edge of the ridge is the gargantuan residence of Bidzina Ivanishvili, resembling something out of a Bond movie with its helipads and futuristic architecture. Ivanishvili is one of Georgia's wealthiest men and served as the country's prime minister in 2012-13.

Now retrace your steps back to the cable car station.

Aerial Tram

One of Tbilisi's newer attractions, just built in 2012, the aerial tram *(Map L, Point 64)* connects Narikala Fortress with the Rike Park just across the river from Gorgasali Square. To ride on it, you need to use a Metromoney card. If you don't already have one, they cost 2 GEL and can be used on any bus and metro in the city. The one-way tram journey then costs 2.50 GEL.

During the ride, you get spectacular views of the entire old town, Mtkvari river, the Bridge of Peace, Rike Park and the Presidential Palace. The lower cable car terminus is inside Rike Park.

Rike Park

Popular with residents and visitors alike, Rike Park stretches along the river from the Presidential Palace to Metekhi Bridge. The most prominent feature within the park is the Concert Hall and Exhibition Centre. This gleaming metallic building has a smooth, tubular design comprising two wings. The northern part is designed to be a music hall seating more than five hundred concertgoers, while the southern portion is an exhibition venue.

Winding paths and picturesque landscaping connect other highlights such as a children's maze, outsized chess boards, dancing fountains and various quirky sculptures one of which is a giant piano. Under the cliff, over which balconies jut out precariously, is a variety of restaurants, and down on the river bank itself are yet more cafes and bars, perfect for a well-earned rest at the end of a day touring Tbilisi.

A short walk across the Metekhi Bridge sees you back in Gorgasali Square where this walking tour ends.

PART 4 - *Exploring east of the Mtkvari River*

This walking tour takes in the sights to the east of the Mtkvari river and begins in the rather grand Marjanishvili Square.

This route can continue from the 'Navigating North from Freedom Square' walking tour. Simply take a red line metro train, one stop from Rustaveli Square in the direction of Akhmeteli Theatre and get off at the Marjanishvili Square station. Or, for those with more time, do the tour on a different day, taking a metro from the station nearest your hotel.

* * *

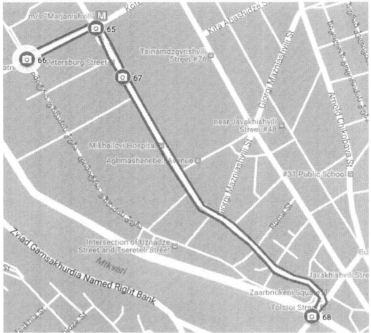

Map M: Marjanishvili Square to Dry Bridge Market

Key:
65. *Marjanishvili Square*
66. *Marjanishvili Theatre*
67. *Davit Aghmashenebeli Street*
68. *Dry Bridge Market*

Marjanishvili Square

Marjanishvili Square *(Map M, Point 65)* is at the heart of the area developed by German colonists during the nineteenth century, and glancing at a map, you will notice how the streets here are laid out on a strict grid layout in true Teutonic style. The square takes its name from Kote Marjanishvili, the celebrated Georgian theatre director famous for his extravagant productions. His theatre is just one block down the road from the square along Marjanishvili Street. By now you should see just how revered this director is, from the number of high profile places named after him.

Walk 150 m down Marjanishvili Street southwest towards the river.

Marjanishvili Theatre

Marjanishvili Theatre *(Map M, Point 66)* is one of the oldest and most important in the country. It was established in 1928 by Kote Marjanishvili in the town of Kutaisi in western Georgia but moved shortly after that to Tbilisi in 1930. It occupied a building that used to be a philanthropic public library set up by the successful merchant brothers Zubaliashvili. Almost a century later the theatre is still going strong. The facade of the theatre is classic art nouveau, and the inside also reflects the iconic designs of the early part of the twentieth century. The main auditorium has seating for more than six hundred people. While almost all productions are in Georgian, the theatre has recently started providing occasional English subtitles for plays. You can check the latest playbill at www.marjanishvili.com/en.

Walk back to Marjanishvili Square and turn right along Davit Aghmashenebeli Street.

Stephen Stocks

Davit Aghmashenebeli Street

This thoroughfare is the main commercial street to the east of the Mtkvari river and handsome, recently-renovated nineteenth-century buildings run along its length *(Map M, Point 67)*. It runs from the area near the Tbilisi Central railway station to Saarbrucken Square.

The street takes its name from the twelfth-century King David IV, popularly known as David the Builder due to his massive construction projects. It is one of the most frequented shopping streets in the whole of Tbilisi and has just undergone a comprehensive revamp. Consequently, most of the buildings lining the street are now sparkling and beautifully-maintained, and the walk along its length is a pleasant stroll indeed.

Halfway along the street, look out for the striking neo-gothic facade of the Mikhailovi Hospital at number 60. Directly opposite the hospital, at number 61, is the old Soviet Propaganda Centre, a 1970s brutalist concrete structure, sporting a colourful mosaic designed by Zurab Tsereteli.

As you approach the end of the street, it becomes pedestrianised. Here, beautiful old balconied buildings line the road, and pavement cafes and bars proliferate. You eventually emerge onto the cobbled Saarbrucken Square at the eastern end of the Saarbrucken bridge.

Dry Bridge Market

Cross Saarbrucken Bridge and you will straight away begin to notice the merchants of the Dry Bridge Market *(Map M, Point 68)*. For anyone who loves a bargain, this is a must-visit place in Tbilisi. Here you can pick up an authentic and quirky souvenir of Georgia, often dating back into Soviet times and beyond. Some people regard this market as a kind of open-air museum, as you see relics of the Soviet era you don't usually see elsewhere.

People love browsing these stalls for old coins, kitchenware, books, vinyl records, vintage appliances and phones, postcards, and just about anything else you can imagine. Negotiation is the order of the day, and as stall holders don't often speak English, a few words of Georgian or Russian would come in handy to make sure you secure a bargain.

The market is open every day, from 10 am to 5 pm, although traders may pack up early in the case of severe weather.

From Saarbrucken Square to St Trinity Cathedral is around 1.5 km, and a short, cheap taxi ride away.

Alternatively, to see a bit more of this part of Tbilisi you can easily walk, although there are some quite long uphill sections. Walk along Leo Tolstoy Street then turn right down Kosta Khetagurovi Street. Continue along the river until you reach the statue of Baratashvili. Climb the steps to the left onto Elene Akhvirediani rise. Walk to the end, turn left and then continue until you reach the cathedral.

* * *

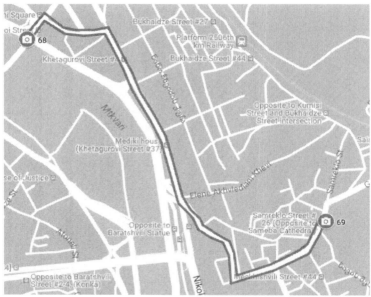

Map N: Dry Bridge Market to St Trinity Cathedral

Key:
> *68. Dry Bridge Market*
> *69. Trinity Cathedral*

St. Trinity (Samebo) Cathedral

St. Trinity, also known as Samebo, is the primary cathedral in Tbilisi for the Georgian orthodox religion *(Map N, Point 69)*. It was completed in 2004 and was built to commemorate 1500 years of the Georgian Orthodox church, and 2000 years since the birth of Christ. With an area of 5000 square metres, it is one of the largest religious buildings in the world. An even the bells are monumental; there is a group of nine with the biggest weighing in at a hefty eight tons.

Its situation at the top of the hill in the Avlabari district means that the church is visible from far and wide. It is built in a traditional Georgian Orthodox style, although it is stretched vertically to a more than 100 m height, giving it a more towering perspective. Opinions are divided, and some regard it as something of an eyesore by some, while others view it as an architectural triumph. You'll have to make your own mind up when you get there.

Inside, the dome is supported by eight impressive columns that appear to reach all the way up to heaven. While not too ornate, you should look out for the beautiful gilded icons that are scattered throughout. There are nine individual chapels each dedicated to a particular saint, some of which are underground. The deepest foundations of the structure include holy materials such as rocks from Mount Sion and the Jordan River, and soil from Jerusalem and St. George's tomb.

The cathedral is just one part of a sprawling complex comprising the residence of the patriarch, a monastery, a separate free-standing belfry, theology school, workshops and even a hotel.

From the cathedral entrance, turn left down Samreko Street and then turn left along Lado Meskhishvili Street. Follow this street all the way to Avlabari Square. Walk to your left across the square, where you will see the sculpture to the actors of Mimino.

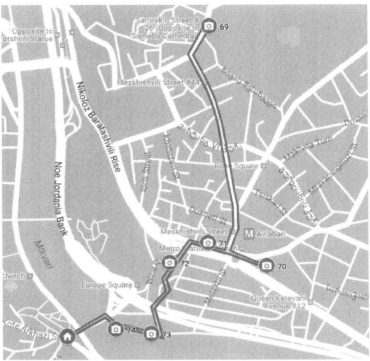

Map O: St Trinity Cathedral to Gorgasali Square

Key:

    69. *Trinity Cathedral*

    70. *Sculpture to the Actors of Mimino*

    71. *Ejmiadzin Armenian Church*

    72. *Queen Darejan's (Sachino) Palace*

    73. *Metekhi Cathedral*

    74: *King Gorgasali Statue*

Tbilisi

Sculpture to the Actors of Mimino

Just across Avlabari Square from the Ejmiadzin church is a whimsical statue celebrating the characters of Mimino *(Map O, Point 70)*, a much-loved 1970s comedy film, written by the very same Revaz Gabriadze who later opened his puppet theatre in Tbilisi. In the movie, a Georgian bush helicopter pilot, Mimino, who dreams of a high-flying airline job, goes to Moscow to pursue his dream. There he meets an Armenian truck driver who was mistakenly lodged at his hotel, and together they have lots of adventures. Eventually, Mimino gets a job flying the Tu144 supersonic jet flying all over the world. However, he ultimately succumbs to homesickness and comes back to the bosom of his family and friends in Georgia.

The sculpture was created by Zurab Tsereteli, the Georgian-born painter and sculptor who founded MoMA Tbilisi.

Walk back across Avlabari Square to the Ejmiadzin Armenian church, which will be facing you.

Ejmiadzin Armenian Church

This Armenian Apostolic church *(Map O, Point 71)* was built in 1804 to serve the local Armenian community. Today, it is one of only two operating Armenian churches in the city, the other being the St. George Armenian cathedral just behind Gorgasali Square.

The church is mostly built from red brick and has a distinctive white drum and dome. Inside, the walls have mostly been whitewashed. To the east of the church, at the end nearest to the metro station, is a superior example of a khachkar, or Armenian stele, showing a carved cross and many elaborate floral motifs. To the side of the church is a curious tall plinth upon which is a small bowler-hatted bust. This statue is a monument to Alexander Mantasgev, a prominent Armenian oil tycoon and philanthropist.

The church was recently the epicentre of an international controversy which blew up from the most trivial beginnings. According to the Georgians, a Georgian woman complained that an Armenian priest's car had blocked her own. When some other Georgians tried to help her, several Armenians attacked them. The Armenians side, however, claimed that the woman verbally and racially abused the Armenians. Fifty people were involved in the clashes. Afterwards, the local Armenian diocese complained, resulting in the Armenian foreign office demanding that the Georgians investigate the 'hate crime'. Some Georgian commentators believe that such overreactions are the result of long-held tensions which were re-ignited following the construction of the St. Trinity Cathedral over part of an old Armenian cemetery.

From the Ejmiadzin Armenian Church, cross the main road. As you dive into the narrow alleyways, take as your landmark the rounded dome and steeple of the Church of the Transfiguration in Queen Darejan's Palace.

Queen Darejan's (Sachino) Palace

The Palace of Queen Darejan *(Map O, Point 72)* is otherwise known as Sachino Palace. Sachino in Georgian means conspicuous, and this proves to be an apt name considering its prominent position overlooking the Mtkheti river and the city. The palace was built in 1776 by King Erekle II on the remnants of the older Alvlabar fortress walls, some of which are still visible today, and the queen used it as a summer residence.

There are two main surviving elements of the complex. The first is a dramatic pavilion perched right on the highest point of the old fortress walls. Circular in shape, the pavilion has a vertigo-inducing wrap-around balcony, from which there are stunning panoramic views of Tbilisi's old town. The second is the Church of the Transfiguration, built at the same time as the palace in 1776. The church has a distinctive tower with an exposed belfry topped by a rounded dome and steeple. While it was used as the private chapel for the Royals, it now serves the whole community.

Queen Darejan was the third wife of King Erekle II, and remarkably their marriage lasted forty-eight years and produced a staggering twenty-three children. She became quite involved in politics and was opposed to the continuing rapprochement with Russia. When her husband died in 1798, her stepson George XII became the new king. George actively sought Russian protection for Georgia and so ratcheted up the conflict with his stepmother. These tensions escalated to such a degree that he confined Darejan to the Sachino Palace. After George died in 1800, the Russians forbade the nomination of a new monarch, prompting Queen Darejan and her sons into open rebellion. Eventually, Tsar Alexander I ordered the deportation of the entire royal family. The queen was deported to Russia in 1803. Following her departure, the site was redeveloped as a monastery and then as a seminary for the children of ecclesiastics.

From the palace, narrow paths will leading to stone staircases descending down the hill towards the river. The steps will eventually emerge near the Metekhi Cathedral.

* * *

Stephen Stocks

Metekhi Cathedral

The Metekhi district is on a clifftop plateau on the eastern side of the Mtkvari river. It's one of the oldest neighbourhoods of Tbilisi. It is said that King Vakhtang first erected a palace and church here in the fifth century and that a Georgian saint, Shushanik, was also buried here. All of these structures were wiped out by thirteenth-century Mongol raiders.

The church you see today *(Map O, Point 73)* was built just after this turbulent period, around 1280. As with most other historical structures in the city, it has been damaged and subsequently renovated many times over. It's a small miracle that the church has survived at all, given that in the Soviet era the communist leader of Georgia, the infamous Lavrenti Beria, proposed to demolish the church. These plans luckily never came to fruition.

The plan of the church is a cross-cupola design, the dominant form of churches in the Middle Ages, particularly in this region. As with the Jvari Monastery just outside of Tbilisi, the spaces between the arms of the cross are filled in, producing a square ground plan. Exterior ornamentation is quite sparse, with architectural flourishes limited to around the windows. Inside, the church has a real atmosphere of antiquity, with its roughly hewn stone walls, icons, and flickering candles. At the weekend, you may be lucky to see a baptism or wedding ceremony.

Tbilisi

King Gorgasali Statue

Next to Metekhi Cathedral is the imposing statue of King Vakhtang Gorgasali *(Map O, Point 74)*, gazing sternly out across the river and old town Tbilisi. This is a fitting end to this walking tour as King Gorgasali is widely credited with founding Tbilisi way back in the fifth century, and many other towns, castles, monasteries and churches.

King Gorgasali is one of the most popular characters from Georgia's long history, and has even been canonised by the Georgian Orthodox Church. He is the subject of epic poems and legends, all of which extol his greatness and courage.

This particular statue of the king, high up on the Metekhi clifftop, was installed in 1967, and designed by Elguja Amashukeli - the sculpter also responsible for the equally formidable Kartlis Deda.

From King Gorgasali's statue, stroll back across metekhi Bridge to Gorgasali Square, where this walking tour comes to an end.

PART 5 - Day trips from Tbilisi

The UNESCO World Heritage Sites of Mtskheta make for a comfortable half-day trip from Tbilisi. The easiest way to get there would be to hire a taxi, and there is no shortage of willing drivers who would be more than happy to take you out there! Of course, negotiate the price before you get in, but depending on your negotiating skills you should be able to get a ride there and back for USD 15-20.

A cheaper alternative is to get a marshrutka. First, take a metro to Didube station. Next to this is the bus station, where you can find the marshrutka. You will need to buy a ticket at the cashier. While this is an excellent option for going to Mtskheta itself, the Jvari Monastery is on a relatively remote hilltop and would require an additional taxi ride to and from town.

If you would like to make a full day trip, you can go around another fifty minutes past Mtskheta to Gori, where there are ancient sites of interest and the Stalin Museum.

— Mtskheta —

Mtskheta, a mere 20 km north of Tbilisi, is an ancient city that has played a central role throughout much of Georgia's existence. In recognition of this religious and historical significance, its monuments, notably the Svetitskhoveli Cathedral and Jvaris Monastery, have been UNESCO World Heritage Sites since 1994. Recently, in 2014, the Georgian Orthodox Church declared Mtskheta a 'Holy City'. Any visit to Tbilisi would not be complete without a day trip here.

The city was the long-time capital of the Georgian Kingdom of Iberia, from the third century BC onwards. It was where Christianity was adopted as the state religion, following St. Nino's conversion of the ruling king in 327 AD. In the sixth century, King Dachi, the successor to King Vakhtang Gorgasali, moved the capital to Tbilisi as it was more readily defended from invaders. Mtskheta nevertheless remained as the headquarters of the Georgian Orthodox Church, and every Georgian king was coronated and buried here, up to the end of the monarchy in the nineteenth century.

The natural setting of Mtskheta is also a draw. It sits in a valley at the confluence of the Mtkvari and Aragvi rivers, surrounded by hilly country. There are lots of old cobbled streets to explore and balconied houses to admire. In the town square outside the cathedral, there are some decent cafes and restaurants, and you can walk lunch off with a pleasant stroll down to the tranquil Mtkvari river.

— Svetitskhoveli Cathedral —

The eleventh-century Svetitskhoveli Cathedral is a masterpiece of Georgian religious medieval architecture. It is said to be the burial site of the robe, known as the mantle, that Christ wore during the crucifixion. The cathedral is undoubtedly the holiest place in Georgia and attracts pilgrims from all over the Caucasus.

In Georgia, 'Sveti' means 'pillar' and 'tskhoveli' translates as 'life-giving'. To find out why the church takes this name we have to look back to the first century AD when a Georgian Jew called Elias visited Jerusalem at the time of Jesus' crucifixion. He bought the robe of Jesus from a soldier and returned to his homeland. When his sister, Sidonia, touched it, she dropped dead from the extreme emotions she felt. She wouldn't let go of the robe, even in death, and so she was buried with it, on the site where the cathedral stands today.

After that, the grave stood alone without any religious buildings erected around it. However, a huge cedar tree grew from her grave, and in the fourth century King Merian, the first king to be converted to Christianity by St. Nino, ordered seven columns to be made, to build a church. The seventh column turned out to have magical powers and rose into the air, and the saint had to pray all night before it came back down to earth. Subsequently, some people spoke of a holy liquid emanating from the pillar which cured any disease, so giving rise to the name Svetitskhoveli. When in the cathedral, look out for the second column upon which a nineteenth-century icon illustrates this story, with Sidonia and an angel lifting the column, and King Miran in the foreground.

The original fourth-century church was built from wood and was superceded in the fifth century by a more sturdy stone structure, the excavated foundations of which are alongside the present-day cathedral.

The cathedral is perfectly proportioned, soaring above the low-lying village of Mtskheta. It is cross-shaped, as you'd expect, with a dome on a tall drum. The structure appears to comprise of a series of stone waves, with the porch, lower nave and upper nave getting progressively higher towards the drum. While the stonework is relatively unadorned, different colours are used for various structural elements; walls are mostly yellow stone, the drum is green, while red stone appears around the apse window. Look out for wine leaf motifs on the western facade as you approach the main entrance. Curiously, on the northern facade, there is a carving of a hand holding a bevel square, allegedly the hand of the architect, Arsukidze. Legend has it that the architect's teacher was so jealous of his masterpiece at Svetitskhoveli that he had his hand chopped off. An inscription on the eastern facade confirms that Arsukidze did not live long enough to see the church completed, but the cause of his death is not known for sure. King Herekle II built the high defensive walls surrounding the cathedral compound in the eighteenth century.

You enter the cathedral from the western door. Immediately on your right is a fourth-century baptismal font, purportedly used for the baptism of King Mirian. Walking down the nave, on the right side, is what appears to be a small stone church. It is a thirteenth-century copy of the Chapel of Christ's Sepulchre in Jerusalem, built to symbolise the position of Svetitskhoveli as the second most holy place in the Christian world due to the presence of Jesus' mantle. In front of the chapel is the grave of Sidonius where fragments of the seventh column remain.

Frescoes originally covered the inside of the cathedral, yet most of these did not survive. In the 1830's Russian authorities whitewashed over them to give the church a 'tidier' look in advance of a planned visit by Tsar Nicholas I which eventually didn't even happen. Today, restoration projects are trying to uncover these, and you can see some thirteenth-century frescoes depicting the 'Beast of the Apocalypse' and various Zodiac figures. The other frescoes and icons visible today mostly date from the nineteenth and twentieth centuries.

Svetitskhoveli played host to all the coronations and royal burials during Georgia's time as a kingdom. Ten kings are believed to have been buried here, but so far only three graves have been found, all arrayed before the altar. The most prominent of these is the tomb of King Vakhtang Gorgasali, fronted with many devotional candles. The eighteenth century King Herekle II is alongside, identified by its sword and shield, and next to his grave is his son King Giorgi XII, the very last king of Georgia.

The cathedral is open daily from 8 am to 10 pm.

— Jvari Monastery —

As with many of the most celebrated ancient churches of Georgia, the Jvari Monastery is perched high up on the top of a small mountain. The sixth-century structure is one of the most visited and photographed in Georgia, and along with other prominent sites down in Mtskheta has been listed as a UNESCO World Heritage Site.

The monastery can trace its origins way back to the fourth century, at which point we meet St Nino again (we saw a replica of her grapevine cross in the Sioni Cathedral in Tbilisi). The saint converted the then-king of the area, Mirian the Third, to Christianity, and afterwards erected a cross on top of the mountain where Jvari monastery now stands. The cross was said to perform miracles, and pilgrims soon came pouring in from all over the Caucasus. In 545, the faithful erected a small church over the remaining fragments of the cross, and the present-day building replaced this in 590. Unusually for historic structures in Georgia, the monastery has by and large escaped the ravages of history, other than some minor damage incurred by Arab raiders in the tenth century. Today, Jvari is very much an active religious site, and on the weekends you might be lucky enough to witness a Georgian wedding ceremony or baptism.

Its design was a first-of-its-kind. While the church's plan is cruciform, the spaces between the arms of the cross shape are filled in with little chapels, making an almost square ground plan. These well-balanced proportions evoke a feeling of tranquillity and harmony, emphasised through the general lack of excessive ornamentation. Outside, the stonework has little carving or other embellishments, although there is a particularly fine bas-relief of angels holding a cross above the south door. Inside the walls are almost entirely bare, making the church feel more spacious and lofty than it actually is.

The classic 1840 poem, the *Mtsyri*, by the celebrated Russian writer Mikhail Lermontov, immortalised the Jvari Monastery. It was supposedly based on a true story he heard during his time serving in the Caucasus as an army officer, whereby a general captured a six-year-old Circassian Muslim boy and left him with Georgian monks at Jvari Monastery.

In its final version, the poem describes the situation of the monastery:

At that place, where
The streams, Aragvi and Kura,
Embracing as two sisters,
Flow together with a roar,
There was a monastery.

The boy found it hard to get used to life in the monastery but seemingly reconciled himself to his fate. Secretly, however, he had never given up hope of seeing his family again, and one day fled the monastery. He spent three days wandering the valley lost, and in the end is found just near the monastery having walked in a big circle. He dies soon afterwards. Mtsyri means novice monk, and the poem shows that the boy, who perished after leaving the monastery, has proved to be just that and no longer Circassian. In other words, nurture, or culture, has prevailed over the boy's nature.

The monastery was built right on the very edge of a vertical cliff, and there is a spectacular view which features on most Georgian postcards. Down below in the valley there is the iconic confluence of the Mtkvari and Aragvi rivers, and nestling in the centre is Svetitskhoveli Cathedral surrounded by Mtskheta.

The site is open daily between 9 am and 10 pm.

— Gori —

Depending on your interest in the history of the Soviet Union, you might consider an extension to the usual Mtskheta day trip. The town of Gori, famed as the birthplace of Joesph Stalin, is less than an hour's drive away, west along the E60 motorway.

Stalin Museum

Remarkably, considering twentieth-century history, and in particular Georgia's repression during the USSR time, the Stalin Museum has remained as a shrine to the infamous dictator. First opened in 1957 shortly after his death, the museum is next door to the house where Stalin was born in 1878.

With its heavy, oppressive concrete structure, the museum

itself shouts Stalinism. Once you are inside the main entrance, you know that you will have an experience unlike any other. A grand marble staircase leads up to an imposing statue of the man himself. The rooms housing the various exhibits are authentically Soviet in decor and ambience.

The artefacts on display are mostly personal items such as the last packet of cigarettes Stalin smoked and his preferred winter coat. Various paintings and photographs document his eventful life. Perhaps the darkest display in the museum, and one most likely to give you nightmares, is Stalin's death mask mounted in a dimly and eerily lit chamber. In the yard of the museum is Stalin's personal train carriage and his childhood house. There is no mention anywhere in the museum of purges, gulags or any other murderous practices.

The museum is open daily between 10 am and 6 pm, and the entrance fee is 15 GEL.

Gori Fortress

Dominating the whole town is the Gori Fortress, an impressive thirteenth-century castle high up on a nearby hill. Due to its strategic importance, it naturally attracted the attention of all invading armies and was captured by the Ottomans in the sixteenth century. After that, it continually changed hands between the Turks, Georgians and Persians. From the battlements are spectacular views of Gori and the Caucasus in the distance.

Due to many battles for control of the castle, much of it has repeatedly been destroyed and then rebuilt. The remaining structure you see dates from the seventeenth and eighteenth centuries, with some of the more visible damage caused by a 1920 earthquake.

Gori was on the frontline yet again in 2008, when Russian

forces occupied the town during its brief invasion of Georgia. In the northeast part of the castle, you can see a sculpture of a circle of mutilated fighters as a memorial to those who lost their lives.

Uplistsikhe cave complex

Uplistsikhe is one of the oldest settlements anywhere in Georgia, founded three thousand years ago in the late Bronze Age. It became an important political and religious centre, and its prominence lasted well into the twelfth century.

Today the remains of the cave complex spread over 40,000 square metres, with the central area containing most of the rock-hewn structures. In addition to regular caves used for accommodation, you can also visit caves used as bakeries, pharmacies, places of sacrifice and even a prison, all connected by tunnels.

Archaeologists have found out that in the pre-Christian era Uplistsikhe residents were engaged in sun worship, and have unearthed many such temples. Upon the introduction of Christianity, the importance of the cave complex dwindled somewhat but continued nonetheless.

Its second heyday came when the Arabs captured Tbilisi, and the Kings of Kartli made Uplistsikhe their residence. Accordingly, the stature of the settlement grew, and it eventually counted 20,000 residents. When Georgians wrestled back control of Tbilisi, Uplistsikhe immediately went into a decline from which it never recovered.

Uplistsikhe is on the tentative list for inclusion on the UNESCO World Heritage Program. So now is the perfect time to visit, before it gains full status and the crowds of tourists start to appear.

Preparing for your visit

— Essential info —

When to Visit

Tbilisi is affected by both continental and subtropical influences. However, as it is bounded by mountain ranges, particularly in the north, it is sheltered from harsh winter weather. The city has a reasonably mild microclimate, and rainfall is spread pretty evenly throughout the year.

Generally, spring and autumn in Tbilisi are cool and pleasant. Summer temperatures are between 20C and 30C but can top 40C in the middle of the day. Winters are cold, and snow falls between 15-25 days each winter.

Visas

Georgia has a relatively relaxed visa regime. More than ninety nationalities are visa-exempt, including those from all

EU countries, the US, Canada, Gulf countries, South Africa, Australia, New Zealand and selected southeast Asian and central and South American countries. Many others can apply for an e-visa online from the official Georgia e-Visa Portal, www.evisa.gov.ge. The cost is USD 20 plus a 2% service fee, and it takes around five working days to process. For all other nationalities, it is necessary to apply for a visa in advance at a Georgian embassy.

Currency

The currency is the Georgian Lari (GEL). Each Lari splits into 100 Tetri. At the time of writing, April 2018, one US Dollar bought 2.40 Lari, one British Pound bought 3.39 Lari, and one Euro got 2.96 Lari. You can easily exchange these main currencies in the city, and exchanges and banks are commonplace. ATMs also accept Visa, Visa Electron, Mastercard and Maestro cards.

Time Zone

Tbilisi is in the Georgia Standard Time (GET) zone, which is GMT+4. The country does not currently observe daylight savings time.

Electricity

Georgia's electricity is of the 220V/50Hz variety. The wall sockets take plugs with two round pins. Take a range of adaptors with you to make sure you can connect.

— Getting There and Away —

By Air

Tbilisi has one airport serving all international and national airlines. Tbilisi International Airport (TBS) is about a 17 km drive southeast of the city centre. It offers a wide range of routes spanning the Middle East, Europe and Russia.

Here are the airlines currently connecting **international destinations** with Tbilisi:

- Aegean Airlines flies to Athens three times each week. www.aegeanair.com.
- Aeroflot has double daily flights to Moscow Sheremetyevo, with onward connections on its services and those of the SkyTeam Alliance. www.aeroflot.com
- Air Arabia links Tbilisi with Sharjah 10 times per week. www.airarabia.com
- Air Astana flies to Almaty and Astana. www.airastana.com
- Air Baltic goes to Riga three times a week.
- Azerbaijan Airlines flies to Baku twice daily. www.azal.az.
- Belavia has daily service to Minsk. www.belavia.by.
- China Southern flies to Urumqi three times a week. www.csair.com
- El Al links Tbilisi with Tel Aviv three times a week. www.elal.com.
- FlyDubai offers flights four flights a day to its Dubai

hub, with onward connections around the Middle East, Africa, the Subcontinent and Europe. www.flydubai.com. Alternatively, passengers can connect to Emirates' global network.

- Georgian Airways offers the widest selection of destinations from Tbilisi, including Amsterdam, Athens, Barcelona, Beirut, Berlin, Bologna, Bratislava, Brussels, Cologne, Kazan, Kiev, London Gatwick, Moscow Vnukovo, Paris Charles de Gaulle, Tel Aviv, Vienna and Yerevan. www.georgian-airways.com.
- Gulf Air goes to Bahrain three times weekly. www.gulfair.com.
- LOT has daily flights to Warsaw with onward connections throughout Europe. www.lot.com.
- Lufthansa has daily flights to Munich. www.lufthansa.com
- Iran Air www.iranair.com, Iran Aseman Airlines www.iaa.ir and Qeshm Airlines www.qeshm-air.com all fly to Tehran, Iran.
- Israir flies to Tel Aviv three times a week. www.israir.co.il
- Pegasus Airlines has daily flights To Istanbul Sabha Gokcen airport. www.flypgs.com.
- Qatar Airways has daily flights to its hub at Doha, from where you can connect to its global network. One of these daily flights also stops off at Baku. www.qatarairways.com
- S7 flies to Moscow Domodedovo. www.s7.ru
- Turkish Airlines has a flight to Istanbul four times most days. From its Istanbul hub, you can fly just about anywhere in the world. www.turkishairlines.com
- Ukraine International Airlines flies to Kiev. www.flyuia.com.

- Ural Airlines serves Yekaterinburg twice a week and Moscow Zhukovsky four times weekly. www.uralairlines.com
- Wataniya links Tbilisi with Kuwait four times a week. www.wataniyaairways.com

As Georgia is quite a small country, there are no air services to other cities domestically.

By Rail

There is a relatively extensive railway network in Georgia, comprising just over 1500 km of track and 22 passenger stations. This comprises a main line running from the Russian border in the northwest to the Azerbaijani border in the southeast, with various lines branching off to major population centres. The most modern double-decker electric trains run between Batumi to Tbilisi. The fare is unlikely to exceed more than USD 15 anywhere in the country.

Tbilisi is connected to several international destinations such as Baku in Azerbaijan and Yerevan in Armenia. In Kupe class, a one-way fare to Yerevan should be around USD 30, and USD 20 to Baku. There is a link to Kars in Turkey, from which the extensive Turkish railway network can be accessed, with connections on to Europe. To travel to destinations in Russia, it is necessary to transit in Baku, as the security situation in Abkhazia has led to the closure of the railway in the border region.

Tickets can be purchased online on the Georgian Railways website, www.railway.ge, although the online booking functionality appears to be only in Georgian. The site also has full timetable and route information, displayed in English. As an alternative, visit the English language ticket booking engine at https://tkt.ge/en/Railway, where you can buy domestics tickets with foreign credit cards.

By Road

There are easy border crossings with Turkey, Azerbaijan and Armenia. Travelling from Russia is more problematic due to the security situations in South Ossetia and Abkhazia.

From Turkey, there are two primary crossings. The first one is at Sarpi on the Black Sea coast and is handy for travellers going to Batumi, a mere 15 km from the border. The other at Vale is more convenient for Tbilisi.

From Azerbaijan, there are two main border crossings. The most direct route from Baku is through the 'Red Bridge' immigration post, a short 70 km drive from Tbilisi. The other option is the Lagodekhi crossing in the extreme east of Georgia.

From Armenia, the southeastern border post at Sadakhlo is conveniently placed on the direct route between Yerevan and Tbilisi. An alternative crossing is at Bavra in southern Georgia.

Travelling from Russia presents more of a challenge. The most straightforward option is to cross the border at Stepantsminda in the Kazbegi National Park. Some travellers report a smooth transit, whereas others are questioned at length by the Russian authorities. So you should be prepared for both scenarios!

By Boat

The main ports of Georgia are Batumi and Poti, and from both there are regular services to Ukraine and Bulgaria.

Ukrferry, www.ukrferry.com, links both Georgian ports with Chornomorsk in southern Ukraine. Large ro-ro ferries operate twice a week in both directions, with the voyage taking about 48 hours. A basic berth costs USD 110 one-way.

There is also an interesting route from Bulgaria, operated by Navibulgar, www.navbul.com, under the brand FerrySped. Their ferry links Poti with Varna, usually once per week. The journey takes 54 hours, and a basic berth costs EUR 110 one-way.

Batumi is linked by fast hydrofoils to Sochi in Russia, by the Express Batumi shipping company. However, this is currently limited to Russians and nationals of other CIS countries.

— Getting Around —

From the airport

Bus 37 runs a service at 12-minute intervals from the airport to the city centre all day from 7 am to 11 pm. Stops include the Rustaveli and Avlabari metro stations and Freedom Square. The fare is 0.50 GED. However, if you are travelling with a lot of luggage, this might not be the best option.

There is an impressive new railway station just a few metres away from the terminal. However, the schedule is quite minimal with infrequent trains in the morning and evening rush hours. The Tbilisi Airport website, www.tbilisiairport.com, has the latest timings.

As most visitors' flights arrive at anti-social hours in the early morning, taking a taxi is often the only practical option. Follow signs for 'Official Taxis' and book with one of the marshalls. The official taxis should cost about USD 20, but you will still need to negotiate well to get that price. As in most places, it is best to ignore the many men offering taxis as soon as you walk out of the terminal.

Around the city

As explained in the detailed walking tours in this guide, the majority of sights are accessible on foot. However, for when feet get tired, or if the weather is not cooperating, the good news is that there are extensive public transport networks.

Tbilisi currently has a two-line **metro** system with a total of 22 stations. The longer red line has sixteen stops, and the green line has six. It runs from 6 am until midnight, and frequencies vary from every two-and-a-half minutes in the rush hour up to ten minutes off-peak. To use the metro system, you first need to buy a Metromoney card for 2 GED, which you can top up with whatever amount you choose. Each one-way ride costs 0.50 Tetri, regardless of length, making this one of the cheapest metro systems in the world. Signs and announcements are in Georgian and English, so it is easy to get around.

Baku's **bus** network spreads its tentacles across the entire city and out into the suburbs. They can take you just about anywhere you want to go. You can either pay on board by inserting the correct coins into a machine or use the Metromoney card. Buses are blue and yellow and display the route number on the front, and most bus stops have screens showing when the next bus is due. For full information in English on buses, including an interactive route planner and timetables, visit the Tbilisi Transport Company website.

Finally, you will see taxis cruising everywhere around Tbilisi, and you can easily hail one from the street. Mostly they are private taxis without a meter, so it is advisable to negotiate the fare before getting in. If you don't speak Georgian or Russia, it would be a good idea to have your destination written down or marked on a map to show the driver. While Uber does not yet operate in the city, a good alternative is the Taxify app.

— Where to stay —

Accommodation in Tbilisi often takes the form of small hotels, apartments and homestays. In recent years, more upmarket boutique style hotels have appeared, along with some of the bigger Western chains. If you are travelling during the peak summer months, you should try to book as far ahead as possible as there can be limited availability during that time. Here are just a few highlights in the top end and mid-range categories, although www.booking.com lists all the possible options at the competitive rates. Furthermore, Tripadvisor.com compares prices with the three or four top hotel consolidators, making sure you get the most reasonable rate. There is also a wide selection of apartments and rooms to rent in Tbilisi on www.airbnb.com.

Top end

Rooms Hotel is a top pick for Tbilisi. Housed in a converted industrial-style building, the beautifully designed hotel has a retro-Soviet style. The location is a bit out of the way, but a nice twenty to thirty minute stroll down Rustaveli Avenue sees you at Tbilisi old town.

Tbilisi Marriott is located right on Rustaveli Avenue near Freedom Square. Classic luxury hotel in a historic building, with all you'd expect including an atrium-style lobby, twinkling crystal chandeliers, marble bathrooms and luxury bedrooms and a range of bars and restaurants.

Radisson Blu Iveria is on the upper part of Rustaveli Avenue, a few steps away from the metro station. This glass-fronted tower has an outdoor swimming pool, and all rooms have great views of either the Mtkvari river or Mtatsminda hill.

Courtyard Marriott directly faces onto Freedom Square, so you can't be more central than that. It has a heated indoor swimming pool and fitness centre.

Holiday Inn Tbilisi is a bit further out past Vera Park but is next to the Technical University metro station. The hotel is housed in a modern block, with an outdoor pool, and is handy for walks along the Mtkvari river.

Mid-Range

Ibis Styles Tbilisi Center is the cream of the crop in this category. Just 150 m south of Freedom Square, this newly-opened hotel is right in the heart of the old city. The hotel has a striking and colourful design throughout, and the highlight is the rooftop open-air bar and restaurant with panoramic views over Tbilisi. Ranked number one on Tripadvisor.

Mercure Tbilisi is a short walk from Gorgasali Square,

Shardeni Street and Abanotubani. This modern four-star hotel comes with spa and sauna, and also boasts a rooftop bar.

Old Tiflis Boutique Hotel is in the Abanotubani area, with Narikala Fortress a mere five-minute walk away. One of the neighbourhood's historic buildings houses this small and characterful hotel.

Shota Rustaveli Boutique Hotel is in a side street off Rustaveli Avenue next to the Georgian Parliament. The interior decor of the public areas and rooms is based on a twelfth-century poem written by Rustaveli himself. A stylish and unique place to stay.

Index

A

B

C

Tbilisi

Zurab Tsereteli Museum of Modern Art 26

Copyright

FewDaysAway

PO Box 215878
  Dubai
  United Arab Emirates

www.fewdaysaway.com

This edition published 2018.

Printed in Great Britain
by Amazon